Edward

1
Ed Sheeran
Self-Portrait, Aged 6
1997
felt pen on paper
29 x 20 cm

This publication has been produced by Ipswich Borough Council
to accompany the exhibition
Ed Sheeran: Made in Suffolk
shown at
Christchurch Mansion, Ipswich, Suffolk, UK
20 August 2019 - 3 May 2020

Published 2019 by Ipswich Borough Council
ISBN 9781916190603 (PB)
ISBN 9781916190610 (HB)
First edition, first print 2019

British Library Cataloguing in Publication Data
A catalogue record for this book is available from the British Library

Photography of artworks by Doug Atfield and Colin Davidson
Designed by Sharon Teague
Printed by Healeys Printers, Ipswich, Suffolk

Exhibition organised by Ipswich Borough Council

Exhibition Team:
John Sheeran, Exhibition Curator
Max Stocker, Project Adviser, Ipswich Borough Council
Jane Wadman, Senior Exhibitions Officer, Ipswich Museums
Emma Roodhouse, Curator of Fine Art, Ipswich Museums
Charlotte de Mille, Education Curator
Helen Pluck, Ipswich Borough Council

Front cover illustration:
Colin Davidson *Ed Sheeran II* 2016, oil on linen (detail)

Back cover illustration:
Mark Surridge *Press Photo Shoot, Chicago* 2017, photograph (detail)

Dedicated to the memory of Ed's grandparents
Shirley Lock (née Walker) 1929-2016
Bill Sheeran 1927-2013

*Profits from the sale of this publication will be
donated to Zest, which provides hospice care for
14-25 year olds with incurable illnesses living in
East Anglia. Zest is part of St Elizabeth Hospice,
Ipswich.*

*This book has been produced by Healeys
Printers, a carbon balanced publications
printer, in conjunction with Ipswich Borough
Council. The book has been printed on carbon
balanced paper and all carbon produced during
production has been offset.*

*This has created 238.43 square metres of new
native woodland and 9.537 tonnes of CO2
captured. As a result of this over 200 trees will
be supplied by the Woodland Trust for Ipswich
Borough Council to plant in Ipswich parks.*

CONTENTS

2
Framlingham, Suffolk
(photo Mike Page)

3
Ed Sheeran, aged 8
Framlingham Castle, 1999
(photo John Sheeran)

4
Ed Sheeran, aged 25
Framlingham Castle, 2016
(photo Murray Cummings)

FOREWORD BY ED SHEERAN

I am so happy to celebrate the end of my two-year world tour with the four homecoming gigs in Ipswich, Suffolk this summer. Suffolk means so much to me. I love walking in the countryside, the open skies, the light, the coast, fish and chips on the beach, or a pint of local beer in an ancient pub. And Ipswich is where I played some of my early gigs before I got signed – at The Drum and Monkey, The Swan, The Steamboat Tavern, McGinty's, and in Christchurch Park for Ipswich Music Day.

I'd like to thank Ipswich Borough Council for coming up with the idea for this exhibition and for asking my Dad to curate it and produce this publication to accompany it. The Council's Max Stocker and I go back a long way. I did my two-week school work experience with him when I was 15. He asked me what I was going to do with my life. I said I was going to be a singer-songwriter touring the world. 'Take my advice, Ed. Stay at school and stick to your exams!' he advised me.

I have always been into art, so I'm really pleased the exhibition includes Colin Davidson. I first met Colin when I played in Belfast in 2014. He's a lovely man and a hugely gifted painter. It was an honour to be drawn and painted by him. I really like the contrast of energy and stillness in his work. It's what my life is all about.

And it's great that Mark Surridge is in the exhibition too. I've known Mark since I first started touring the UK, when I was a support act for Example. We got on really well. He is a photographer you hardly notice.

He just quietly gets on with his job, taking beautiful photos of what you experience in an arena or stadium – on the stage, in the crowd or behind the scenes. He is also a superb portrait photographer.

My Dad has uncovered all sorts of stuff, going way back to my childhood and teenage years. He seems to have kept everything – even my very first song lyrics, when I was about 13. I'm glad he did.

I am happy that the exhibition has exciting creative activities for young people, including portrait painting, photography, songwriting and music workshops. I am also thrilled that proceeds from this project will help to raise funds for much-needed Zest teenage hospice care in Ipswich.

I am grateful to everyone who has worked on the exhibition and this publication. Thank you Ipswich, and thank you Suffolk.

THE MAYOR OF IPSWICH

I am proud and pleased to welcome Ed Sheeran to Ipswich for the biggest musical experience the town has ever seen. I also have the pleasure of introducing this impressive exhibition, which will, I am sure, attract an audience not only from Ipswich and Suffolk but across the UK and beyond. It is also of huge cultural significance to the town.

Ed's story is well known but many pictures and sculptures in *Ed Sheeran: Made in Suffolk* are on show for the very first time. Thanks to the curation of Ed's father, John Sheeran, this is an intimate portrait of a singer-songwriter who revels in his roots and who is proud of both town and county.

Ed Sheeran has come such a long way from the days of busking in the town and playing in front of a few dozen people in local pubs. This exhibition is a road map of that journey.

My thanks to Ipswich Borough Council colleagues, to Colin Davidson and Mark Surridge, John Sheeran, Brad Jones of Archant and to Aspall for making it happen.

Councillor Jan Parry

THE SPONSOR

It is an honour to be the exclusive partner to this exhibition. Just like Aspall, Ed is fiercely proud of his Suffolk roots and we are delighted that this exhibition will help shine a light on our beautiful county.

Aspall has been making cyder and vinegar in Suffolk since 1728, and our family has a long history of taking the road less travelled to get to where we are today. Ed could have ended his tour anywhere, but he chose Ipswich, proving a passion for Suffolk and integrity that we as a brand share.

The Borough were clear that they wanted a true 'Made in Suffolk' brand to support this exhibition and after 300 years of making cyder from the same spot in Suffolk, we are pleased that they thought Aspall had enough experience to fit the bill!

We have a lot to be proud of in Suffolk but are not always good at shouting about it. We hope that this exhibition will be the start of something very exciting for our region and that Suffolk will become even more celebrated for first-class music, food, drinks, art and culture.

Cheers, Suffolk!

Henry Chevallier Guild
Founding family member and Aspall board advisor

5
Martin guitar used by
Ed Sheeran, 2008-11

ED SHEERAN MADE IN SUFFOLK

ED, ART & MUSIC

by John Sheeran

6
Ed Sheeran's hand
unused cover design for
The Orange Room EP, 2005
(photo John Sheeran)

ED, ART & MUSIC

Ed Sheeran, aged 1, 1992

8
Ed Sheeran's childhood Lego

My wife Imogen and I worked for many years as art curators, organising exhibitions, producing art publications and advising professional artists. We chose to bring up our two children, Matthew and Edward, in as fertile a creative environment as possible, with minimal access in their early years to TV, and without computer games. There was a lot of drawing, painting, cutting, pasting and sticking, dressing up, story-telling, singing, dancing and music-making with drums, whistles, cymbals and homemade instruments. The kitchen was covered with their art, and there was also an old piano which they bashed and banged away at. So from early on, the boys saw being creative as a natural part of everyday life, and as fun. Most of all, Ed enjoyed playing with Lego, and he still does today (8). Imogen also dressed the boys in vibrantly coloured clothes, which seemed to me to perfectly express their warmth, happiness and positivity (7).

We also went on long walks, encouraging the boys to look closely at nature. They gave us their own guided tours, like mini-David Attenboroughs. Their imaginations ran wild as they described the bugs, butterflies and sticklebacks. They had their own names and we were told vivid stories about their lives and families. Ed has since talked to us about the impact that all this creativity had on him. A prime example is the way he has had his own body tattooed, turning it into a remarkably personal ongoing artwork and colourful visual diary of the key memories, moments and influences in his life (9). It is hardly surprising that art features so prominently on his skin, from Van Gogh and Matisse to Basquiat and Damien Hirst.

9
Ed Sheeran 2017
(photo Greg Williams)

10
Ed Sheeran and Damien Hirst with spin paintings for
the ÷ *(Divide)* album cover work, 20 October 2016
(photo Damien Hirst Studio)

ED, ART & MUSIC

We have always had artists coming in and out of our house - painters, sculptors, printmakers, photographers, textile artists and ceramicists. We got into the habit of commissioning portraits of the boys from artists we knew and admired. Some of their work is included in the exhibition and illustrated in the following pages. Alan Flood was the first. He drew three extremely fine drypoints for us back in the 1990s, including one that showed us as a family group above Hebden Bridge in West Yorkshire, shortly before we moved to Suffolk (13).

Shirley Fraser, whom we asked to do a bronze sculpture, had the most difficult task. It is a miracle she managed successfully to model - in clay, from life - two small boys who could never stay still. We turned their bedroom into a studio, so she could work all day while they played around her. The resulting piece is a poignant study of early childhood and brotherly love, and over the years it has given Imogen and myself a warm inner feeling whenever we look at it (16).

Martin Yeoman painted sensitive portraits of our boys in 2002, in his Wiltshire studio and at our house in Framlingham. Martin has such a fine and delicate artistic sensibility. The portrait of Ed, aged 11, has a beautiful, timeless innocence about it. It perfectly captures a boy on the cusp of adolescence (17).

The Colombian artist, Cristina Rodriguez, whom we were advising, painted a colourful, joyous five metre frieze-like painting for us in 2004, with bold, simplified forms (19). It includes Matthew playing his violin, Edward his guitar, and Imogen dancing with a pink flower in her hand. I am sitting with a book in a walled garden, with Framlingham church behind. The castle and mere feature on the far right.

In 2007, Laurence Edwards produced fine, strong busts of both boys, after several sittings in his studio at Butley Creek, Suffolk (21). I have long thought that Laurence is one of the UK's finest figurative sculptors and it is heartening to see that Ed takes such a keen interest in his work. He recently visited him in his studio in Halesworth, Suffolk, to talk to him about his new sculptures, including the massive bronze figure *Suffolk Man*, which will be installed at Yoxford in 2021.

And the family art tradition continues. In 2015, Ed welcomed the Northern Irish painter Colin Davidson into his Suffolk home. Three superb drawings, five oil studies and two large portraits resulted. The National Portrait Gallery, London, later acquired one of the large portraits (126), and the remaining pictures, never seen before, feature in the exhibition and are illustrated in this book.

Since Ed's career took off in 2011, he has been photographed by hundreds of photographers around the world but there have only been a handful who have been there from the beginning. Mark Surridge is one of them. In preparing the exhibition, Mark and I looked through a thousand of his photographs of Ed, whittling them down to a mere 18. Mark is self-taught and a natural, and he knows the music scene inside out, having been a roadie and tour manager when Ed was starting out. He has an instinct for the right moment and the right shot, whether before, during or after a performance.

11
Alan Flood
Matthew and Edward Sheeran 1992
drypoint print
21 x 14 cm (plate mark)

12
Alan Flood
Matthew and Edward Sheeran 1992
(detail)
drypoint print
21 x 14 cm (plate mark)

13
Alan Flood
Sheeran Family, Hebden Bridge 1995
drypoint print
18.5 x 30 cm (plate mark)

14
Alan Flood
Matthew and Edward Sheeran 1998
drypoint print
19 x 19 cm (plate mark)

A/P — Matthew and Edward Sheehan   Flood 98

15
Ed Sheeran, aged 3, at home with sculptor
Shirley Fraser, Hebden Bridge, West Yorkshire
September 1994
(photo John Sheeran)

16
Shirley Fraser
Matthew and Edward Sheeran 1994
bronze, unique
48 x 41 x 32 cm

17
Martin Yeoman
Ed Sheeran 2002
oil on canvas
45 x 30.5 cm

18
Ed Sheeran with artist
Martin Yeoman in his studio
East Knoyle, Wiltshire
16 August 2002

19
Cristina Rodriguez
The Sheeran Family 2004
oil on linen
157 x 548 cm
(not in exhibition)

20
Ed Sheeran, aged 16, with sculptor
Laurence Edwards, Butley Creek Studio
Suffolk, 13 November 2007

21
Laurence Edwards
Ed Sheeran 2007
bronze, limited edition of 2
37 x 19 x 24 cm

ED, ART & MUSIC

Ed's homecoming gigs in Ipswich in August 2019 provide a fitting climax to his gruelling ÷ (Divide) world tour, in which he played 260 gigs in arenas and stadiums over two years to more than eight million people. The choice of Ipswich shows just how important his Suffolk roots are to him. As Max Stocker from Ipswich Borough Council said to me recently: 'Ed was made in Suffolk.' It is so true. The Ipswich gigs are the largest cultural event in the history of Ipswich and Suffolk. More than 150,000 people are expected to visit over the four days of the gigs.

Ed has called his track *Castle on the Hill* a 'love song for Suffolk' and he has a deep affection for the landscape and its people. So Max and I decided that the exhibition and this publication should include a record of his Suffolk years. I have selected some of our private family photographs and ephemera relating to Ed's creativity throughout his childhood and teenage years. It is also fascinating to look at the local and regional press coverage of Ed from 2008 to the present (107). It has been unfailingly supportive and positive. Brad Jones, Editor of The East Anglian Daily Times (EADT), has put together an excellent video on loop for the exhibition, showing photos and articles about Ed and his career. They capture so well the growing local excitement and pride in his achievement over the years.

The East Anglian Daily Times, established in Ipswich in 1874 and a media partner for the exhibition project, is also producing a special commemorative issue on Ed's homecoming. Aspall Cyder, established in Suffolk in 1728 and the exhibition sponsor, has arranged a fascinating display on their Suffolk heritage at Christchurch Mansion, Ipswich. It is great

22
Ed Sheeran, aged 13
busking, Galway, Ireland
7 August 2004
(photo John Sheeran)

to see how Ipswich Borough Council, the EADT and Aspall have come together to support the exhibition. Ed was 'made in Suffolk' and the entire project has been produced in Suffolk too. Ed's manager, Stuart Camp, and the UK Kilimanjaro Live promoter, Stuart Galbraith, are also from Suffolk.

The exhibition and this publication include photographs of key moments of Ed's early musical development. There is the first time he went busking, aged 13, in Galway, Ireland (22), and his first ever session in a recording studio, in Leiston, Suffolk, aged 14 (26-29, 36). There is also his first ever public gig, in 2005, at the Royal British Legion, Framlingham, Suffolk (31). I kept the gig flyer (30), ticket and Ed's setlist, and these are all included in the exhibition. Remarkably, that evening Ed sang 40 songs, which included covers of his favourite artists, from Dylan and Clapton to Damien Rice and Nizlopi, some performed as duets with his school friend, Ruby Farr.

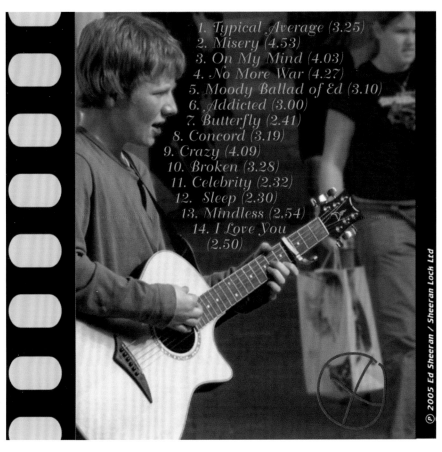

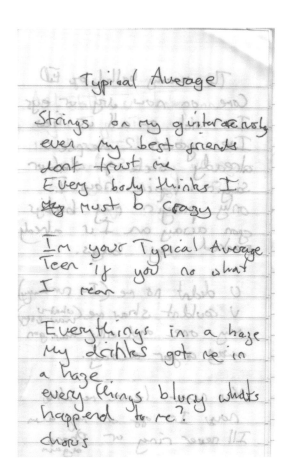

23
Back of *Spinning Man* CD, 2005
(photo by John Sheeran)

24
Handwritten lyrics, aged 13
for *Typical Average*, 2004

Thomas Mills High School

Music Department

Instrumental/Vocal Report 2003- 2004

Name. Edward Sheeran .... Form. 8 JE .... Instrument. Voice ......

Progress and achievement during the year

[handwritten] Ed is a natural performer- brilliant. Obviously at the moment his voice is beginning to change altho' he still has quite a lot in his higher register. Ed has made good progress & is learning to work more with the others as a team. I particularly enjoy this guitar/voice work, its great to be entertained in a lesson! Nice to know what it is all about. I think he can already 'hold' an audience. Well done boy!

Areas for development

[handwritten] Keep working on listening to the others. Develop the band & with solo work. (Don't lose your love of music, listen to all sorts)

Extra-curricular/ area / county ensemble involvement

Signed........ *[signature]* .... Instrumental/Vocal Tutor

25
Ed Sheeran music report, aged 13
Thomas Mills High School, Framlingham
Suffolk, summer 2004

26-29
Ed Sheeran, aged 14, in a
recording studio for the first time
with Henry Readhead, Summerhill
School, Leiston, Suffolk
12 March 2005
(photo John Sheeran)

26

27

28

29

30
Poster for the first public gig by
Ed Sheeran, aged 14
16 April 2005

31
Ed Sheeran at his first public gig
duetting with friend Ruby Farr
Royal British Legion, Framlingham
Suffolk, 16 April 2005
(photo Steven Coates)

ED, ART & MUSIC

There are also photographs in the exhibition of Ed's first pop video shoot, aged 15, which was made free of charge by the Bruizer Creative Video Agency at their studio at Bentwaters, near Woodbridge, Suffolk (32, 33, 35). My favourite photo of Ed performing in his early teenage years is one I took at the Moon and Mushroom pub festival at Swilland, Suffolk, when he was 15 (34). It is mid-afternoon. Ed is performing on a lorry-trailer stage. Bales of straw have been left out for people to sit on. Ed is so bottom of the bill that no one has turned up yet, apart from a small child, who is more interested in the chair Ed has used to climb on stage, than the music. It is an amusing acorn moment in Ed's career as a performer. I have also included a photograph of Ed and his mates from the Class of 2007 at Thomas Mills High School (42) and of his Year 11 Prom *Most Likely to be Famous Award*, from the same year (43).

I have put into the exhibition one of Ed's early music reports, taken from his second year at Thomas Mills High School, when he was 13 years old (25). It describes him as 'a natural performer – brilliant .... he can already "hold" an audience.' Richard Hanley, the Head of Music, takes such a refreshingly positive approach to music education. He considers each pupil on their own merits, as a vessel full of creative potential, needing individual encouragement and nurturing for them to flourish. Richard and his department do not have a one-size-fits-all approach, and they are not fixated by exam results. The diversity and quality of the Thomas Mills High School concerts and musicals that Imogen and I attended over the years were outstanding. We would always leave the school feeling uplifted, thankful and fortunate.

Richard instantly picked up on Ed's innate creativity and passion and encouraged him to explore his own musicality in whichever way he wanted. There were plenty of opportunities to do this – at school concerts, recitals, charity gigs, musicals and plays. The music rooms were also made available for pupils to use in their own time. Ed is forever grateful to Richard Hanley and he has acknowledged his impact many times in interviews. Richard is naturally modest, saying that the school only creates the right environment and atmosphere for each pupil to thrive – but in a time of exam-obsessed education, that is some achievement. Ed has been back to the school quite a few times since he left. He is keen to pass on to current pupils what he has learnt about songwriting and the music industry. Imogen and I were also delighted that he gave free tickets for his final gig of the ÷ *(Divide)* world tour to all the current pupils and teaching staff at Thomas Mills High School. I can only imagine the aspirational impact of seeing one of the school's former pupils performing in front of 45,000 people.

As a teenager, Ed was a real grafter when it came to practising the guitar, learning about recording studio processes and performing as much as he could to get experience. I remember seeing his fingers bleeding badly from cuts made by guitar strings, yet he would still carry on. His dedication and determination were remarkable. There is a photo I took of him with his acoustic guitar in his bedroom, which he had converted into his own mini-studio (38). We often heard sounds of guitar playing and singing through his door, as he recorded hour after hour. There is also a shot I took of him with his excellent - and patient - guitar teacher, Keith Krykant, a jazz guitarist who lived locally (36).

32
Ed Sheeran, aged 15, recording his first ever video, for his song *Open Your Ears*, at Bruizer, Bentwaters Park near Woodbridge, Suffolk, 16 August 2006 (photo John Sheeran)

33
Screenshot of Ed Sheeran's video for *Open Your Ears* 16 August 2006

34
Ed Sheeran, aged 15, performing at *Moon Fest*
Moon and Mushroom pub Swilland, Suffolk
27 August 2006
(photo John Sheeran)

35
Ed Sheeran, aged 15, recording at Bruizer
Bentwaters Park, near Woodbridge, Suffolk
16 August 2006
(photo John Sheeran)

36
Ed Sheeran, aged 14, with his guitar teacher,
Keith Krykant, at the Summerhill School
recording studio, Leiston, Suffolk
12 March 2005
(photo John Sheeran)

37
Ed Sheeran, aged 14, at one of his first professional
recording sessions, with producer Julian Simmons
Din Studio, Limehouse, London, 11 December 2005
(photo John Sheeran)

38
Ed Sheeran, aged 14, in his bedroom studio
Framlingham, Suffolk, 2005
(photo John Sheeran)

When he was 14, Ed recorded for the very first time in a professional studio, with the producer and sound engineer, Julian Simmons, who ran the small-scale Din Studio in Cable St, Limehouse, London (37). We went there many times over a couple of years. Ed and I would get up at 6am on a Saturday and drive from Suffolk to the East End. Ed would then record at Din from 9am to 8pm, with only the occasional break, while I got on with my own work. We stayed overnight at a bed and breakfast in Bethnal Green and then returned to the studio for another full session on the Sunday. We would drive back to Suffolk late at night and Imogen and I would make sure he was up in time for school on Monday morning. He was like a sponge when it came to learning about music, recording and performing. We would be back down at Din Studio the following weekend for another intense two-day session. Songs just flowed from him. It was extraordinary to witness.

The exhibition includes a group of shots by local professional photographers who covered the live music scene in Ipswich, Norwich and elsewhere, when Ed's star was rising in East Anglia. Andi Sapey photographed Ed as a 16 year-old performing with his 'backpacker' guitar at the Norwich Playhouse in 2007 (39, 40). Those were the days when Ed wrote his setlist on his forearm. You can see that he has written 'New Song.' This was the first time he sang *You Need Me*, later to become a hit. I think it was after this particular gig that Imogen and I were contacted by Ian Johnson who ran Access to Music Norwich. He had been to the gig and was the first person to pick up on Ed. He gave Ed and ourselves much-needed advice about the next possible stages in Ed's development and career, and has been a constant support over many years.

I have also included the first ever article on Ed, when he was 15, written by his school friend, Steven Coates, which was published in 2006 by the Suffolk Norfolk Life magazine (41). It includes a photograph of Ed taken outside Ipswich Corn Exchange when he was off school on a two-week work-experience programme with Max Stocker, who ran the Communications Department of Ipswich Borough Council. During this time, Max asked Ed to write an article about the Ipswich music scene in the Council's Ipswich Angle newspaper, which is where the photograph was first reproduced.

Talent-Ed
By Steven Coates

Over the past twelve months, Suffolk boy, Ed Sheeran began recording his first album at a large studio in London. Ed wrote thirteen songs for his debut at the Din Studios in Cable Street between October 2005 and March 2006.

Ed, aged 15, lives in Framlingham with his older brother and parents. The Thomas Mills High school student first picked up a guitar in 2002 and began to amaze his family and friends with the speed and skill at which he was learning. To start off with Ed learnt covers of his favourite songs by his idols such as Bob Dylan. Soon after, he decided to delve into his own mind and write his own music. Following much pen-to-paper scribbling Ed finally finished his first song, Typical Average. It tells the story of him growing up and being a, "typical average teen," as the lyrics set out. He has written over 30 others since then.

Showing great enthusiasm towards music and learning the guitar, Ed was given a professional recording system, allowing him to record all his music in his own bedroom. With all the songs that the budding musician had written he decided to produce his own album. Ed started to record his songs at his home in 2004 and produced a fourteen track sampler called Spinning Man, which came out in January 2005 for friends and family to buy. Encouraged by the response from his school friends, Ed chose five tracks to work on for his first professional CD, The Orange Room EP. All the music was recorded by Ed at the Summerhill Studios, Leiston, in March 2005. Through the success of all this, Ed's parents' company set him up with a website, www.edsheeran.com and in June 2005 following his first solo gig in April his music was played on the radio. Moody Ballad of Ed, the first track from the EP was broadcast for people to hear his talent.

Living the normal life of a teenage boy, Ed has written thirteen new songs for his first professional album whilst studying hard for his GCSEs. In Ed's spare time and at weekends his parents travelled up to London with him to work hard at the Din studios with a producer and sound engineer named Julian Simmons who helped Ed bring his musical creations to life. The album was released at the end of June '06 and is available to buy from his website and other shops.

The keen musician has benefited greatly from the support of his friends, family and the teachings of three guitarists based in Suffolk - Dave King, Graham Littlejohn and Keith Krykant. He has also had the honour to have been taught by Preston Reed, one of the USA's greatest guitarists. Hoping to follow in the footsteps of other singer-song writers such as Damian Rice and James Blunt, Ed's future is definitely looking bright.

Ed strumming in the studio

SUFFOLK & NORFOLK LIFE July 2006

41
First ever article on Ed Sheeran Suffolk Norfolk Life magazine July 2006

42
Ed Sheeran, aged 16, Class of 2007
Thomas Mills High School
Framlingham, Suffolk

Thomas Mills High School
Year 11 Prom Award
Most Likely to be Famous
Presented to:
Edward Sheeran

May 2007

43
Most Likely to be Famous,
Year 11 Prom Award
Thomas Mills High School
Framlingham, Suffolk
May, 2007

ED, ART & MUSIC

There is also a photograph of Ed winning The Next Big Thing Grand Final in Norwich (45). For the first time, Ed began to attract interest from the regional media. In April 2009, he won the Soundwaves Ultimate Band Contest, at the Seckford Theatre, Woodbridge. Word spread fast and Ed soon began to develop a significant fanbase from gigging incessantly. Imogen and I knew little about how the music scene worked, but in those early years we tried to help Ed practically as much as we could. We drove him around from gig to gig, created and ran his edsheeran.com website (54), produced his CDs (56), created his merchandise (55) and manned the sales desk at his gigs whenever we could. It was exciting to see him progress in Suffolk from playing at local parties and youth clubs to pubs like The Anchor in Woodbridge, or The Steamboat Tavern and The Swan in Ipswich, where there might be 50 to 100 people to see him. I remember a couple of great nights at McGinty's Irish pub in Ipswich.

Jen O'Neill's photographs for the local and regional media, capture the excitement of this period. My favourite of these is a photo Jen took in The Swan of Ed singing *You Need Me* with the Ipswich rapper Scott French joining in (50). It perfectly captures the party atmosphere of those pub gigs. You can see that Ed is having such a great time. He loved the intimacy of those nights, with the audience right up close, joining in, shouting out and cracking jokes. Sadly, The Swan closed but is set to reopen this summer. McGinty's changed hands and was rebranded. The Drum and Monkey, another Ipswich pub Ed played in, near Ipswich Town Football Club, was recently demolished. The Steamboat Tavern, run by Val Bint when Ed played there, has survived.

Ipswich, of course, is Ed's local town and not that far from where he grew up in Framlingham. After leaving Suffolk for London, whenever he came back he would gig locally. This included at Ipswich Music Day, a huge free public music festival, which takes place every summer at Christchurch Mansion in the park. I well remember the buzz his performance created in 2008 when he first played there to around 200 teenagers on one of the small stages. When he returned in 2010, he was on a much larger stage (47). It is fitting, then, that the *Ed Sheeran: Made in Suffolk* exhibition should take place at Christchurch Mansion, which provided Ed with such an important early platform for his talent. There is now a stage at Ipswich Music Day named after Ed, which showcases young, up-and-coming regional talent.

Imogen and I then witnessed Ed progress to clubs and larger venues in Norwich and London. I remember our sales desk at The Waterfront, Norwich, being swamped by fans. We could not cope with the scramble, so we asked friends who were attending the gig with their daughters to help. One of the last times we helped Ed out was at The Bedford pub, Balham in October 2010. He had the show recorded and filmed for a self-released CD/DVD. There was an incredible atmosphere. That night we knew Ed's career was going to take off.

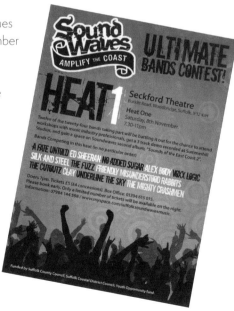

44
Poster for Heat 1 of The Ultimate Bands Contest
Seckford Theatre, Woodbridge, Suffolk
8 November 2008
later won by Ed Sheeran

45
Ed Sheeran, aged 17, winning The Next Big Thing
Grand Final, University of East Anglia, Norwich
9 November 2008
(photo Angela Sharpe, Archant)

46
Poster for
The Next Big Thing
Grand Final, 2008

47

48

49

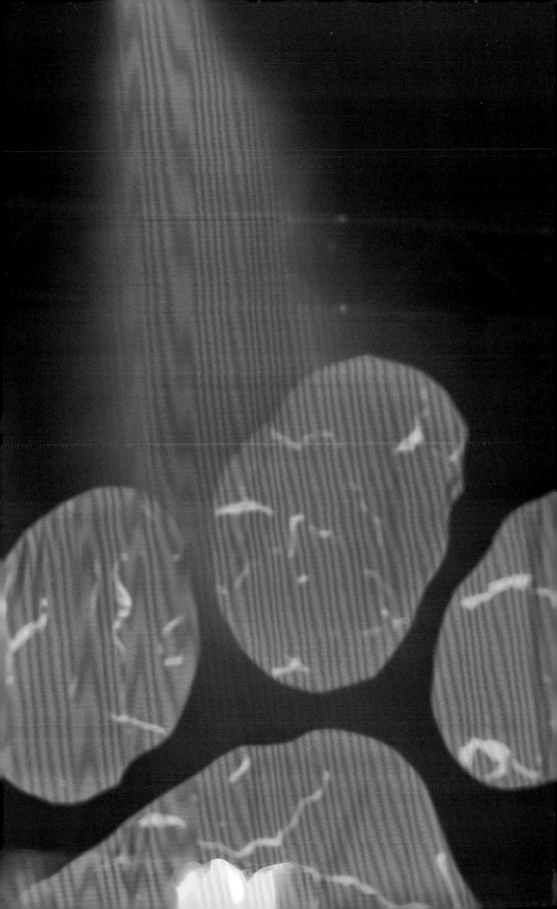

helpdesk » | my account » | my basket »

Shop

News & Live Dates

Resources

Links

Mailing List

Contact

PRODUCT SEARCH

WANT SOME? ALBUM

Ed's second album, 2007

from £0.79

ED SHEERAN ALBUM

Ed's first album, 2006

from £0.79

THE ORANGE ROOM EP

Ed's first CD, 2005

from £0.79

ED SHEERAN T SHIRT

from £9.99

Ed Wins The Next Big Thing

Singer-songwriter Ed Sheeran has been named as the Next Big Thing in the music world at the annual East Anglian band contest.

Under New Management

Ed has been managed since the beginning of 2008 by Crown Music Management in London. Ed is represented by Chloe Griffiths and Jono Ball. Click on headline to read more...

Ed Gigs

3 December 2008 at 8:00PM Access to Music Awards' Ceremony, The Mayfair Theatre, London **4 December 2008 8:00PM** T Bird, Arsenal, London **6 December 2008 8:00PM** Acoustic Sessions @ The Ivy House, London with Stephen Long **9 December 2008 at 8:00PM** Electro Acoustic Club @ The Slaughtered Lamb, London **12 December 2008 at 8:00PM** Music Born @ Zenith Bar, London **14 December 2008 at 8:00PM** The Queen Charlotte, Norwich **23 December 2008 at 8:00PM** The Vinyl Club @ The Steam Boat, Ipswich **27 December 2008 at 8:00PM** Mr Wolf's Noodle Bar, Bristol Click on headline to read more...

New Photos by CCPHOTOART.biz

Ed recently spent a great day in London in the company of photorahers Patrick Cusse and Christie Goodwin aka CCPHOTOART.biz.   Click on headline to read more...

Ed Sheeran

Welcome to the website of UK singer-songwriter Ed Sheeran, where you can buy his albums, Eps and individual tracks, as well as T-shirts, wrist bands and badges. You can also listen to his music, read his lyrics, look at photos, watch videos of him performing, and find out about up-coming gigs. If you would like to contact Ed or book him for a gig, then you can do so via the Contact page of this website.

Mailing List >

Keep up with the latest news, including advance notice of gigs and new releases >

site by Turtle Reality

54
Ed Sheeran website
December 2008

55
Ed Sheeran merchandise, 2007

Spinning Man 2005

The Orange Room EP 2005

Ed Sheeran 2006

Want Some? 2007

You Need Me 2009

Loose Change 2010

Songs I Wrote with Amy 2010

Let it Out 2010

Live at The Bedford 2010

No.5 Collaborations Project 2010

Total Physical and Download Sales
2005 - 2010
30,000

ED, ART & MUSIC

Ed always loved painting and drawing. I have included a self-portrait drawing he did with a felt pen, when he was six (1). He has a wide smile, his eyes are lit up and he is waving to us. The drawing expresses the joyful simplicity and purity of childhood. I think it also captures Ed's innate positivity, which has helped him to overcome hurdles throughout his life, from bullying at school to repeated rejection by the music industry in the years after he left Suffolk.

The confident brushwork in a small landscape painting he did in 2001, when he was 10, reveals just how at ease he was in expressing himself creatively at such a young age. The picture shows a view across the lake, or mere, at Framlingham Castle, with the sun setting (58). I remember him painting it. He did not do it at the castle, but at home, from his imagination. He knew the castle and mere so well, as it was his playground for years. The picture is more an impression of the scene than an accurate view. There is also a photograph I took of him, aged 11, painting one of the many pictures he did in our kitchen (57). This one he called *Two Sides to Every Story* (59). It expresses with vibrant colour and bold imagery his feelings about happiness and grief, and the stark contrast between the positive and negative in life - themes which he later explored in his songwriting.

There are also examples of work from his school GCSE Art portfolio. These include a 16 year-old self-portrait, inspired by Andy Warhol, painted in acrylic in the distinctive orange and black colour scheme which soon afterwards he made his trademark (60). I have also included in the exhibition original artwork for some of the 10 self-produced EPs and albums he wrote and recorded between the ages of 14-19,

before he signed to Asylum Records (61-65). As a Christmas present from us in 2010, Imogen arranged and framed all these CDs for him (56). He has since told us that the present is one of his most prized possessions. In the years when he slept on people's floors and sofas, playing hundreds of gigs, most of them unpaid, he lived off the proceeds of selling these CDs from his rucksack.

57
Ed Sheeran, aged 11, painting
Two Sides to Every Story at
home, Framlingham, Suffolk
March 2002
(photo John Sheeran)

58
Ed Sheeran, aged 10, *Framlingham Castle Mere* 2001
gouache on paper, 12.5 x 26 cm

59
Ed Sheeran, aged 11, *Two Sides to Every Story* 2002
mixed media on paper, 25 x 30.2 cm

60
Ed Sheeran painting an acrylic self-portrait for his GCSE Art
portfolio, Framlingham, April 2007 (photo John Sheeran)

58

59

60

61

Ed Sheeran, aged 16, artwork for *Want Some?* EP 2007, ink and pen on paper, 23 x 17.5 cm

62

Ed Sheeran, aged 18, artwork for *You Need Me* EP 2009, biro on paper, 29.8 x 20.5 cm

63

Ed Sheeran, aged 19, artwork for *Loose Change* EP 2010, mixed media on paper, 21 x 29.7 cm

64

Ed Sheeran, aged 19, artwork for *Songs I Wrote with Amy* EP 2010, felt pen on paper, 21.1 x 21.5 cm

65

Ed Sheeran, aged 19, artwork for *Let it Out* single 2010, felt pen on paper, 21.1 x 21.5 cm

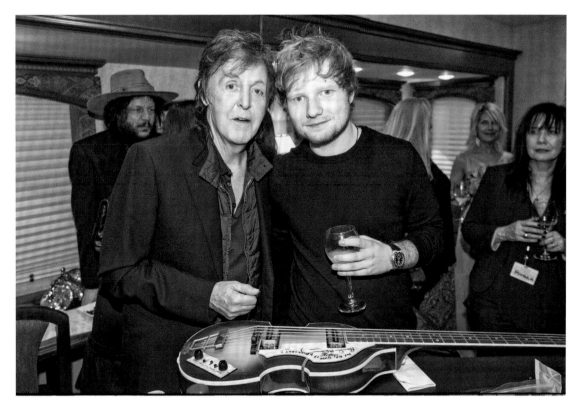

66
Paul McCartney
and Ed Sheeran
after performing at
*The Night That
Changed America:
A Grammy Salute
to the Beatles*
Los Angeles
Convention Center
7 January 2014
(photo MJ Kim)

Revisiting all this material has released a flood of memories for Imogen and myself. We can still see Ed and Matthew as children, standing in the pulpit of St Michael's Church, Framlingham, at a choristers' concert, singing alternate verses of *Where Have All the Flowers Gone?* There is also Ed standing in the church organ loft at a Christmas service singing solo the first verse of *Once in Royal David's City*. Or Ed, aged 10, performing his Eminem-inspired *Criminal* rap at a school recital. I remember many parents looking confused, wondering what on earth was coming out of his mouth. And Ed, aged 11, wanting to take up the guitar after watching Eric Clapton on TV, playing *Layla* at the Golden Jubilee Concert at Buckingham Palace. Then there is Ed, not long afterwards, at his godmother Claire's birthday party in Hemel Hempstead, being taught his first guitar chords by our friend, Hazel May.

We then started taking Ed to gigs to experience some of the British greats. It was wonderful to see Ed, aged 12, at a Paul McCartney gig at Earls Court, singing away to Beatles songs. Then came Eric Clapton at the Albert Hall, and Elton John at Portman Road, Ipswich. How extraordinary that he now knows all of them. Elton John has been an invaluable mentor for years. I remember our excitement watching Elton perform with Ed for the first time, in Los Angeles at the 2013 Grammys. Elton had tried to get Ed a slot to play at the ceremony but the organisers said he was too little known. So Elton offered to play *The A Team* with him to get over that hurdle. Eric Clapton has likewise become a friend. He recorded a guitar solo for one of Ed's tracks and Ed has performed on stage with him at the Budokan, Tokyo. Eric also presented him with the Ivor Novello Songwriter of the Year in 2018. What a moment for Ed - and us.

67
Poster with Ed Sheeran as a support act for Just Jack, Shepherd's Bush Empire
9 November 2009

68
Letter to Ed Sheeran from the Academy of Contemporary Music, Guildford
listing his failure in all music subjects, 31 August 2010

Ed Sheeran ✓
@edsheeran

Follow ⌄

Having lunch with just jack today, without that guy I would not be where I am now, true talk, he's helped me out more than I realise

2:59 AM - 27 Aug 2010

69
Ed Sheeran tweet about Just Jack,
27 August 2010

ED, ART & MUSIC

But if I had to choose one moment that sums up the almost surreal nature of Ed's life - and by proxy, ours - it would have to be the evening of 7 January 2014 at the Los Angeles Convention Center, which Imogen and I attended. Ed had been asked by Paul McCartney to perform at *The Night That Changed America: A Grammy Salute to the Beatles,* which celebrated the 50th anniversary of the Beatles on *The Ed Sullivan Show.* Ed performed the John Lennon song *In My Life,* solo to an audience which included Paul, Ringo, and the Beatles' families. Afterwards, Ed met Paul in his dressing room and asked him to sign a 1962 Hofner bass guitar, as a memento of a special evening. Paul wrote on it 'For Ed who is brilliant!' The guitar is now a treasured possession of Ed's. Paul asked his photographer MJ Kim to take a shot of them together and we now have it hanging at home as a special reminder of a great experience (66).

When I look back at Ed's development as a songwriter and musician and at his career, and try to work out what the key turning points were, there are several candidates. His favourite band in his mid-teens was Nizlopi. They took him on as a guitar tech for the summer holidays, when he was 15. He has acknowledged them as a huge early influence on his music and performance style. As already mentioned, Ian Johnson of Access to Music was the first to spot his talent, at the Norwich Playhouse in 2007, and to act on it. Winning The Next Big Thing competition in Norwich in 2008 gave him a super boost in confidence. At the time, he was attending the British Academy of New Music (BANM) in the East End of London, where he became absorbed by the Grime and Hip hop scene, and had free time to record and gig as much as he could.

He also loved being part of the IKTOMS collective of singer-songwriters, especially when he toured with them around the UK.

However, it was a London songwriter friend, Lester Clayton, who was the catalyst for Ed's first big break. Lester had been asked by Just Jack to be his support act for his UK tour in late 2009. Selflessly, he told him that he should take Ed instead. At the time, Ed had just started at the Academy of Contemporary Music (ACM) in Guildford. Just three weeks into the course, and already disillusioned with it, he asked his tutors for permission to go on the tour but they refused. He then rang us to say that he was determined to go, even if it meant him leaving college. Neither of us were surprised. Ed was developing a fearless gut instinct. Imogen and I caught up with him supporting Just Jack at the Shepherd's Bush Empire (67). Ed's soon-to-be manager, Stuart Camp, was also there. The following August, Ed showed us a letter he received from ACM (68), which included his final results: Fail for Musicianship and Fail for Songcraft – hardly surprising as he never returned.

70
Poster for Example gig at The Waterfront, Norwich, 10 May 2010 when Ed Sheeran was a support act

71
Jamal Edwards and
Ed Sheeran, SBTV
photo-shoot, London
31 January 2011
(photo Jack Young)

A few months later, Jamal Edwards, founder of SBTV, featured Ed performing *You Need Me,* which went viral. Jamal and Ed formed a close relationship and have been good friends ever since (71). Just two months later, in April 2010, Ed flew to Los Angeles for a month, funded by his rucksack CD sales. He performed his first gig at the *Flypoet Spoken Word & Music Showcase* in Inglewood. This was another key moment in his career. It is worth watching his performance on YouTube, where someone has commented, '19 years old and has been in the states (sic) for about a week and walks into a predominantly black audience in friggen Englewood (sic) and sets it on fire.' Ed's name spread quickly and he was asked to play numerous gigs in LA, including at the Foxxhole,

which led to him appearing on Jamie Foxx's radio show, and to staying at Jamie's home, with unlimited use of his recording studio. Ed returned to England incredibly fired up by his American experience. Soon afterwards, Example took him on as a support act on his UK tour (70). Ed's career gathered a new-found momentum and he immersed himself in writing and recording, producing five CDs that year.

There are many memorable Ed occasions which Imogen and I have been fortunate to experience since then: Ed signing his six-album deal with Asylum Records in January 2011 was the first. Typically, he chose to sign not at a swish choreographed event in London, but in Framlingham, Suffolk – at his local pub,

ED, ART & MUSIC

The Station (72). He told us he wanted the Asylum record executives and his lawyer to understand where he was from, to meet his parents, and to experience Suffolk, even if only briefly.

Then there was his first album + *(Plus)* going straight to No 1 in the UK charts in September 2011, which we all celebrated afterwards in a pub in Clapham. I remember seeing tears in the eyes of Ed's manager, Stuart, and realising then just how much his work with Ed meant to him, and how committed he was. I believe theirs is one of the great artist-manager relationships of the British music industry. Ed later gave us a plaque for the + *(Plus)* album going five times Platinum (74). It is now one of the longest charting albums in UK chart history.

In April 2012, we flew to Washington to see Ed perform at the 9:30 Club as the support act for Snow Patrol on their *Fallen Empires* tour. We arrived to find that Ed had turned a tiny dressing room into a mini-recording studio. We found him writing songs with Johnny McDaid of Snow Patrol, which they then played to us. Seven years on and they are still writing together. After his set that night, Ed and I went backstage to meet his agent, Marty Diamond, for the first time. I remember Ed asking Marty how long it would take before he could play Madison Square Garden. Marty disguised his incredulity very well. Like Marty, I was thinking 'But you haven't even done a headline tour of your own yet!' Incredibly, the following year, Ed sold out three nights at the 'The Garden', aged 22.

72
Ed Sheeran signing
a six-album deal
with Asylum Records
The Station pub
Framlingham, Suffolk
17 January 2011
(photo Alex Fairfull
Archant)

73
Poster for Ed Sheeran at Madison Square Garden 2013

Imogen and I sat, all nerves, in the stands in front of Buckingham Palace for the Queen's Diamond Jubilee Concert in June 2012, when Ed sang *The A Team* to tens of thousands in the Mall, and millions on TV. We were lucky to be there too when Ed performed just a couple of months later at the London Olympics Closing Ceremony, singing Pink Floyd's *Wish You Were Here* with Pink Floyd's drummer, Nick Mason, Mike Rutherford from Genesis and The Feeling's Richard Jones.

For a large chunk of 2013, Ed was in the States, based mostly in Nashville while he supported Taylor Swift on her *Red Tour*. This opened him up to a new young American audience. Ed also got to experience everything involved in taking a major show on the road. And he has never forgotten just how important those Just Jack, Example, Snow Patrol and Taylor Swift support tours were for him. He has since taken many young acts on tour with him throughout the UK, Europe and worldwide.

74
Plaque presented to Ed Sheeran by the British Phonographic Industry to recognise 1,500,000 sales of the album + *(Plus)* 2011

ED, ART & MUSIC

For his birthday present in 2014, Imogen and I commissioned the Bristol-based graffiti mural artist Graham Dews (aka Paris) to paint a large six-canvas work to celebrate Ed's career to date (76). The canvases intriguingly fuse the Framlingham Castle skyline, and those of Los Angeles and New York, with impressions of three of Ed's favourite concert venues: Radio City Hall, New York; Madison Square Garden; and the Ryman Theatre, Nashville. The logos of Flypoet, SBTV and Asylum Records are superimposed on the lower tier. We first met Graham in 2005, when he worked with us on art education projects in schools around the UK. He stayed with us in Framlingham and helped design the Ed Sheeran album of 2006. It was Graham who chose the American typeface Mom's Typewriter for the 'Ed Sheeran' logo, which has been used ever since. He also spray-painted a canvas portrait of Ed with his guitar which hung in Ed's bedroom during his teenage years (75).

63

76
Graham Dews (aka Paris)
Birthday Present for Edward 2014
spray-paint on six canvases
200 x 453 cm

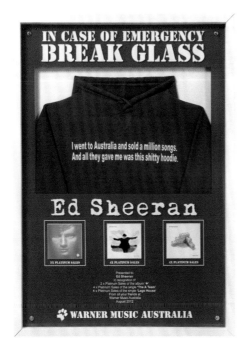

77
Plaque to mark + (Plus) going
2X Platinum in Australia, 2012

Ed has received numerous plaques from record companies, promoters, venues and music industry organisations around the world. They record all his major career milestones. My favourites tend to be the ones that are creative or amusing. In 2012, Warner Music Australia presented him with a plaque to mark the + (Plus) album going Double Platinum (77). It contains a blue hoodie printed with the words 'I went to Australia and sold a million songs, and all they gave me was this shitty hoodie.' In 2013, he was presented with a superb plaque made out of Lego to celebrate + (Plus) going Platinum in Canada (78).

The UK promoters, Kilimanjaro, create particularly imaginative plaques. To celebrate his first gig at the O2 in London, they presented him with his old loop pedal deconstructed, laid out piece by piece (79). Ed's USA promoter, the Messina Touring Group, gave him a plaque with a circle of tickets for every one of the 55 shows of his sold out tour (80). The plaques seem to be getting bigger and bigger. The Recording Industry Association of America recently gave him a suitably grand piece to celebrate two million sales of the ÷ (Divide) album (84). Ed has also been presented with numerous music awards, from the Brits and Ivor Novellos, to BBC Music, Q and MTV, to the Billboards and Grammys, some of which he has generously loaned to the Ipswich exhibition (85-92, 94).

78
Plaque to mark + (Plus) going
Platinum in Canada, 2013

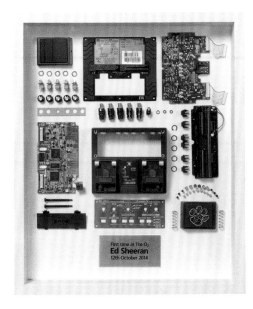

79
Kilimanjaro Live gift to mark Ed Sheeran's
first gig at the O2, London, 2014

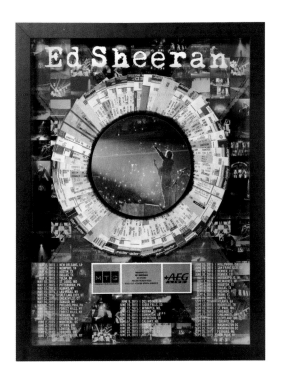

80
Messina Touring Group & AEG gift
to mark the end of the 2015 USA tour

81
Kilimanjaro Live and DHP Family gift to celebrate
three sold out shows at Wembley Stadium, 2015

82
Recording Industry Association of America plaque
to mark X (Multiply) going 2X Platinum, 2015

83
Recording Industry Association of America plaque
to mark Thinking Out Loud going 5X Platinum, 2015

85   86   87   88

89   90   91   92

85
British Artist of the Year, BBC Music Awards, 2014

86
Brit Award, 2015

87
Grammy Award announcement opened by Stevie Wonder, 2016

88
Artist of the Year, MTV Video Music Award, 2017

89
Global Recording Artist of 2017, International Federation of the Phonographic Industry

90
Best Act in the World Today, Q Awards, 2017

91
Songwriters Hall of Fame, David Starlight Award, 2017

92
Top Artist, Billboard Music Awards, 2018

93
YouTube presentation to celebrate Ed Sheeran passing One Million Subscribers, 2013

94
Ed Sheeran's Ivor Novello and Grammy awards, 2012-2017

There are also numerous gig and tour posters. I think my favourite is from June 2015. Ed rang us at short notice to say that Mick Jagger had asked him to be the support act for the Kansas City show of the Rolling Stones *Zip Code* North America tour. Within a couple of days, we were in our seats watching Ed live. During the Rolling Stones set, he came on stage to duet with Jagger on *Beast of Burden*. It was a spine-tingling moment for parents who grew up in the Sixties. Shortly after we arrived home, a package from Ed arrived – we opened it to find a Rolling Stones Kansas City gig poster signed and dedicated to us by the Stones (95). I have, of course, included that poster in the exhibition.

Ed has worked on numerous pop videos with many outstanding directors, such as Emil Nava and Jason Koenig. In 2015, Ed asked me to work with Emil on the video for his song *Photograph*. It involved an intense couple of days in a studio in Soho, London, fast-forwarding through 60 hours of family videos, saving numerous clips, later edited, that show Ed from the age of six months through to his late teens. It was extraordinary to experience a life flashing by on screen like that. The video perfectly captures the sensation of a life passing by in minutes, as Ed progresses from a baby lying on our bed to walking on stage to play to thousands of people at a festival.

The previous year, Emil Nava directed the video for *Sing*, which shows a caricature puppet of Ed on a night on the town. The slightly creepy puppet was used again in 2018 for Emil's video for *Happier*. Ed has kindly lent it to the Ipswich exhibition (96).

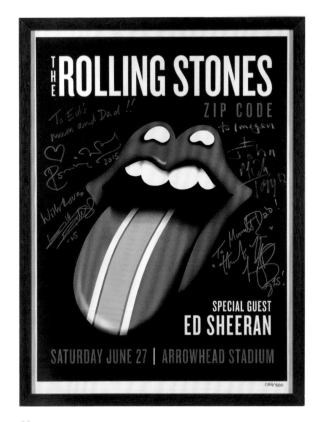

95
Poster for the Rolling Stones *Zip Code* gig at The Arrowhead Stadium, Kansas City signed by the Rolling Stones and given to Ed's parents, 2015

96
Caricature puppet of Ed Sheeran
used in the official videos
for *Sing* (2014) and *Happier* (2018)

There have been films too. *Jumpers for Goalposts* was shot at Wembley Stadium during his three solo shows in 2015. *Songwriter* (98), directed by Ed's cousin Murray Cummings, came out in 2018. It covered the writing and recording of the ÷ *(Divide)* album in the States and the UK.

More recently there has been the Richard Curtis and Danny Boyle homage to the Beatles film, *Yesterday* (99), much of it filmed in Suffolk. Richard Curtis, who has a house in Suffolk not far from Framlingham, has known Ed since he was about 17. He has seen him grow from playing small local venues to becoming a global star. Richard explained in interviews at the time of the film's launch how the experiences of Ed and his local girlfriend inspired the love story in the film.

98
Songwriter film poster, 2018

99
Yesterday film poster, 2019

ED, ART & MUSIC

In July 2019, Ed released his fourth album, *No 6 Collaborations Project*. I think the whole venture helped keep him sane during the grind of the second half of the ÷ *(Divide)* world tour. He loved the challenge of cross-fertilising his creativity with that of artists of widely differing music genres; some well-known, others less so. As he travelled across states, countries and continents, he always had something to look forward to musically and creatively.

I remember an early discussion about the project in 2018, in the basement of Gymkhana, one of Ed's favourite Indian restaurants in London. Ed, Steve Mac and Johnny McDaid were all celebrating getting an Ivor Novello Award earlier in the day for their work on *Shape of You*. Max Lousada, Chairman of the Warner Music Group, was also there and he and Ed got chatting away. Ed has always valued Max's take on things and floated the idea of a collaborations album similar to the concept of *No 5 Collaborations*, which he had worked on with UK Grime and Hip hop artists years earlier, before he ever got signed. Max was really enthusiastic and within minutes Ed was like an excited schoolboy, brainstorming possibilities of potential collaborators. 'I've come across so much talent on my travels, I'd love to work with some of the people I rate and like,' Ed said. He considered the *No 5 Collaborations* album as one of the most creative and satisfying music projects he had ever worked on. 'The UK Grime scene has to feature on *No 6*,' he emphasised.

The one track from *No 6* that I was most interested to hear was Ed's collaboration with Eminem and 50 Cent. When Ed was around 10 years old, my brother Jim recommended we get him the *Marshall Mathers LP*.

Jim said Ed would enjoy Eminem's wordplay, his lyrical wit and the sheer energy of his storytelling. Imogen and I knew nothing of Eminem, but got the CD for Ed anyway. Within a few days, Ed was rapping Eminem's lyrics with no hint of the stammer he had suffered from for years. We were astonished.

Ed made a point of inviting Jim, Imogen and myself to Twickenham Stadium in summer 2018 to see him perform *River* with Eminem. It was their first time on stage together. Ed met 50 Cent in Eminem's dressing room that day and hatched the idea of a collaboration among the three of them. The track, *Remember The Name*, opens with Ed name-checking Ipswich. 'No one ever sings about Ipswich or Suffolk,' I said when I first heard it. Ed just smiled. 'That's the whole point,' he said, 'I think it's cool, I want Eminem, and 50 Cent, and everyone else to know where I come from.' I was really pleased that Ed saw Ipswich as just as real or relevant as anywhere else; indeed, more so for him individually, as the town is an indelible part of his own personal history.

100
Ed Sheeran with UK Official Charts awards for No 1 Album *(No 6 Collaborations Project)* and No 1 Single *(Beautiful People)*, 19 July 2019

101
÷ *(Divide)* tour poster,
Ipswich 2019

ED Sheeran

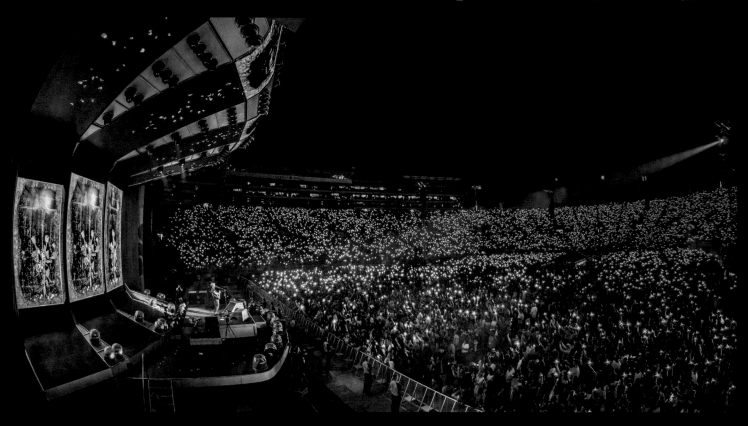

FRIDAY 23 AUGUST	SATURDAY 24 AUGUST	SUNDAY 25 AUGUST	MONDAY 26 AUGUST
IPSWICH	**IPSWICH**	**IPSWICH**	**IPSWICH**
CHANTRY PARK	CHANTRY PARK	CHANTRY PARK	CHANTRY PARK

 VISIT EDSHEERAN.COM FOR FAQ'S   THE ALBUM ÷ OUT NOW

I Love You
(Ed Sheeran 2004)

I'm standing on a mountain
Waiting for you to come
You were sitting counting
The days that I had gone
The note I wrote
I wrapped up in a cigarette
Burned away the memories
I tried to forget
But not yet

Wishing my life away
But these three words
I have to say to you
My baby blue
You know it's true
I love you
I love you

How can I tell you?
I don't know what to say
This chance that I won't miss
But I miss you anyway
I feel your pain
It's turning me insane
Thrown away
I had to take the last train home

But then you came
Wishing my life away
But these three words
I have to say to you
My baby blue
You know it's true
I love you

Wishing my life away
These three words
I have to say to you
My baby blue
You know it's true
You know it's true
I love you
I love you
I love you

Ed Sheeran: vocals, acoustic,
electric and bass guitar, drums

www.edsheeran.com

SHEERAN LOCK

Inside spread:
'Touch' by Phil Robbins, 2005
oil on canvas

The Orange Room EP
Ed Sheeran

102
I Love You lyrics
The Orange Room EP
2005

I want to end with a favourite memory and a couple of favourite photographs. The memory is of Ed, aged 13, coming downstairs in his pyjamas to sing us one of his first songs, *I Love You*. It was such a special moment. He sang completely at ease and full of feeling. Then off he went back upstairs, no doubt to write some more songs. He later recorded *I Love You* for *The Orange Room EP* 2005 (102), by which time his voice was struggling with the changes that take place in early adolescence. It is an EP he stopped selling, as it was too much of an embarrassment for him.

There are two photographs that mean more to Imogen and myself than perhaps all the others. They are reproduced here, opposite. One shows Ed on the day he joined Framlingham's St Michael's Church church choir, aged six (103). His brother Matthew holds him close. This is where it all started for both of them: one now a classical composer, the other a singer-songwriter. Alongside, is a photograph taken almost 20 years later by Mark Surridge (104). Matthew and Ed are together again, this time at Abbey Road Studios, in St John's Wood, London, where the Beatles created

their great albums. The boys have just completed the recording of *Perfect* with an orchestra. This was the first time they had ever worked together; it had been the dying wish of Imogen's mother. She got to see film of it later that day and died not long afterwards. It meant a great deal to her, as this is where she too had recorded – as Shirley Walker - a classical singer. Indeed, she is the family link with Suffolk, as she sang at the Aldeburgh Festival under Benjamin Britten from the early 1950s and decided to retire there.

After visits to Aldeburgh to see Imogen's parents, Shirley and Stephen, we would stop off at Framlingham Castle on the way back to Yorkshire. The boys loved to play there. It was a ploy to get them so tired they would sleep all the way home. Once in 1995, we said to them that we were thinking of moving to Suffolk to live near Granny and Grandpa. We asked them where they would like to live. They both shouted from the back of the car, 'We want to live where the castle is! We want to live where the castle is!' So that settled it. We moved to Framlingham, with its castle on the hill. And Suffolk became their home.

103
Ed, aged 6, on his first day in
the choir at St Michael's Church
Framlingham, Suffolk, with his
brother Matthew, 20 April 1997
(photo John Sheeran)

104
Ed Sheeran with his brother
Matthew, at Abbey Road Studios
after recording the orchestrated
version of *Perfect*, 5 August 2016
(photo Mark Surridge)

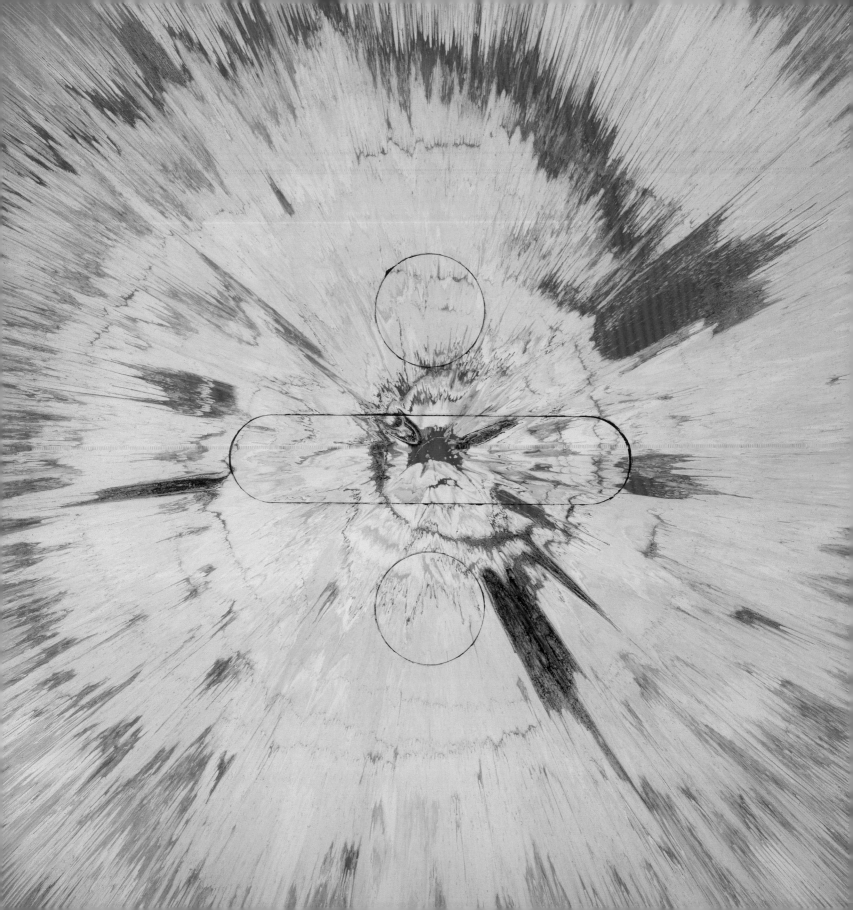

105
Ed Sheeran ÷ (Divide)
Spin Painting No 1 2016
acrylic on canvas
183 x 183 cm
(produced in Damien Hirst's
studio)

When I was 6 years old I broke
my leg

I was running from my brother
and his friends
Tasted the sweet perfume
of the mountain grass I rolled
down
I was younger then
Take me back to when

I found my heart and
broke it here
Made friends and lost
them through the years
and Ive not seen the
roaring fields in so long
I know I've grown
but I can't wait to
go home

I'm on my way
driving at 90
down those country lanes
singing to Tiny Dancer

and I miss the way
you make me feel

its real
when
we watched the
sunset over the

castle on the hill

15 years old and
smoking hand rolled
cigarettes
running from the law
through the back fields
and getting drunk
with my friends
had my first kiss on
a friday night
I don't reckon that I
did it right but I was
younger then
Take me back to when

We found weekend jobs
and when we got paid
We'd buy cheap spirits and
drink them straight
Me and my friends have
not thrown up in so long
oh how we've grown
I can't wait to go home

One friend left to sell
clothes

One worked down by the
coast

One has 2 kids and
lives alone

Ones brother overdosed

Ones already on his
second wife

Ones just barely getting
by

These people raised me

I cant wait to go home

106
Ed Sheeran
handwritten lyrics for
Castle on the Hill

LOCAL PRESS CUTTINGS 2008-2019

Press articles selected
by Brad Jones, Editor
The East Anglian
Daily Times, Archant
Community Media Ltd

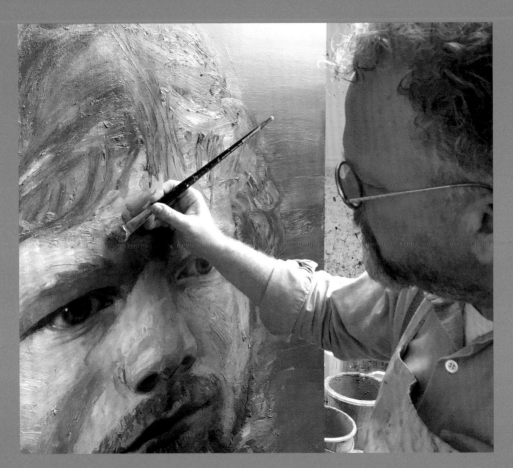

108
Colin Davidson touching up
Ed Sheeran II 2016 in his
studio, Bangor, near Belfast
Northern Ireland, 2019
(photo John Sheeran)

ED SHEERAN MADE IN SUFFOLK

PORTRAITS

by Colin Davidson

Colin Davidson is a contemporary artist, living and working near Belfast, Northern Ireland. His portraits have won widespread acclaim and many international awards. His sitters have included Seamus Heaney, Brad Pitt, Sir Kenneth Branagh, President Bill Clinton and Queen Elizabeth II. Colin's portraits are in numerous public collections, including the Ulster Museum in Belfast, the National Gallery of Ireland in Dublin, The Smithsonian National Gallery in Washington and the National Portrait Gallery in London.

109

110

111

109-111
Ed Sheeran with Colin Davidson at his
home in Suffolk, 14 August 2015
(photos John Sheeran)

PORTRAITS BY COLIN DAVIDSON

On 9 October 2014, I drove my mother, Anne Sheeran, from Wexford, where she lives, to Belfast to see her grandson Ed perform at the Odyssey Arena. We stopped off at the Culloden Hotel, on the outskirts of Belfast, for an early evening meal with the former British athlete and Olympic gold medalist, Dame Mary Peters, one of my mother's closest friends, before we all made our way to the Arena. Mary talked about the Belfast painter Colin Davidson, who had just completed a portrait of her. She was going to see it for the first time the following day, in the artist's studio in Bangor, a few miles away, and she invited us both to go with her. I am used to visiting artists' studios, but it was a first for my mother. Colin took us into a room below his studio to show us the painting. Mary smiled the smile she has in the portrait and my mother said, 'That's you exactly. He's caught your spirit.'

I later asked Colin why he had chosen Mary as a subject and he told me that, growing up in Northern Ireland during the Troubles, Mary was an iconic presence and symbol of hope. 'For decades she has been a uniting force in a divided place. We are all proud of her - for her humanity and decency, and for bringing our community together. She has shown that there is good in us. In my portrait, I wanted to get beyond the façade of the public figure to the human being behind. That is what my portraiture is about.' This struck a deep chord in me: portraiture not as mere visual description, but to capture the essence of an individual; a thinking, feeling, sensitive being. Colin mentioned that he would like to do the same with Ed.

Colin also told me his two daughters played Ed's tracks repeatedly in the car on the morning school run. He said he felt he knew Ed well through his songs.

112
Ed Sheeran with Colin Davidson at his home in Suffolk, 14 August 2015 (photo John Sheeran)

PORTRAITS BY COLIN DAVIDSON

So I suggested he come with his wife and daughters to Ed's second gig in Belfast that night. At the after-show gathering, I introduced him to Ed. You could see the two get on immediately. Ed knew several of Colin's musician sitters, including Glen Hansard, Lisa Hannigan and his good friend Gary Lightbody from the band Snow Patrol. Later, Ed said he would be happy to sit for a portrait by Colin.

Colin told me how fascinated he had been by Ed's live performance at the Odyssey, playing on his own and building up his sound, layer upon layer through loops. He likened Ed's musical artistry to his own painterly technique. He too puts down layer upon layer - of paint. A picture can take him weeks or even months. With Ed, it is all done live and in an instant: putting down a beat, developing the structure, adding melody for feeling, and finally singing or rapping for meaning. Colin said he was amazed. If he makes a mistake with his painting, he can just scrape it off, or paint over it. But for Ed, there is no room for error.

It took many months to find a day when Ed was free for Colin to visit. He arrived in Suffolk from Belfast on 14 August 2015 with his sketching equipment and camera. He was happy for me to be present. I took a few inadequate photos during the session, some of which are reproduced here (109-112). Colin later told me that his portrait sittings always tend to start with a period of uneasiness between artist and sitter. 'There is something intense and unsettling about having someone sitting in front of you, so close, intimately studying every part of your face.' You can see this tension in one of the photos I took, as Ed nervously looks across at Colin sketching. The moment soon passed.

114
Colin Davidson touching up
Ed Sheeran II 2016 in his studio
Bangor, near Belfast
Northern Ireland, 2019
(photo John Sheeran)

113
Ed Sheeran II 2016
on an easel in
Colin Davidson's
studio, Bangor
near Belfast
Northern Ireland
2019

115
Colin Davidson
Ed Sheeran Portrait Study 1
2015
Conté crayon on paper
79 x 59 cm

PORTRAITS BY COLIN DAVIDSON

During his childhood and teenage years, Ed became accustomed to posing for artists, and he has sat for numerous photographers throughout his professional career. I think he was surprised to hear Colin say that he did not want him to pose in any way. 'Wear what you like. Sit where you like. Do what you like. I want it to be as natural as possible.' So over the next couple of hours, while Colin worked, Ed lay on a sofa reading, looking at his laptop, watching the TV or just thinking. Colin later commented, 'I want the sitter to be as relaxed as possible, so they become unaware that I am present. I want to look at Ed as he appears to me, in that moment; not as he might appear to his fans. I knew after a while I would get a reflective Ed; and eventually I would get a daydreaming Ed.'

Colin produced some 25 lightning-fast pencil sketches in front of his sitter. His process reminds me of Turner dashing off scribbled drawings wherever he went, creating his own visual shorthand which holds key elements of a composition. Back in the studio, Turner's visual jottings served as triggers to his phenomenal visual memory. Colin's approach is similar, though his erratic line is more reminiscent of an abstract expressionist's mark-making. He did not seem to be describing anything in particular, such as the shape of a nose or an ear. His pencil marks were produced to remind him later of what he saw in the moments he made those marks.

Colin also took photographs during the session, to record form, colour and light. He said he would use these to compare the likeness to the heads he would create in the studio.

During the sitting, Ed and Colin had a fascinating conversation about stammering. Both had stammered since early childhood. Ed described how he had been born with a port-wine stain birthmark by his left eye, for which he received laser treatment from the ages of two to six. The treatment was very painful, so an anaesthetic cream was applied liberally and locally before the laser zapping took place. During one visit, by mistake, the anaesthetic was not sufficiently applied. The pain of the treatment was intense. From then on he stammered. Colin and Ed spoke of the misery of their early schooldays - being taunted and bullied - and of the frustration of not being able to realise their thoughts in words. Ed spoke of learning to rap Eminem's *Marshall Mather's LP* lyrics when he was 10, and of the miracle of finding he did not stammer at all. They both agreed that their experiences growing up, though uncomfortable, had helped to fuel their self-determination and desire to prove themselves in other ways. I could sense a growing bond between the two artists, based on a mutual respect for each other's creativity and the challenges they had faced.

Colin later told me what a joy it was to be working on something that had no agenda, no specific outcome, no deadline, no fee – indeed, it did not even matter if there was no painting to show at the end. Being given complete artistic freedom, he said, always led to his best work: 'I can do what I want, when I want - or not at all.' He said that with understanding sitters like Mary Peters and Ed, he could work with a refreshing singularity of purpose. He said he came away from the visit to Suffolk determined 'to trap in the painted surface the spirit of the time we spent together.'

116
Colin Davidson
Ed Sheeran Portrait Study 1
2015 (detail)
Conté crayon on paper
79 x 59 cm

117
Colin Davidson
Ed Sheeran Portrait Study 2
2015
Conté crayon on paper
79 x 59 cm

118
Colin Davidson
Ed Sheeran Portrait Study 3
2015
Conté crayon on paper
79 x 59 cm

119
Colin Davidson
Ed Sheeran Portrait Study 2
2015 (detail)
Conté crayon on paper
79 x 59 cm

120
Colin Davidson
Ed Sheeran Portrait Study 3
2015 (detail)
Conté crayon on paper
79 x 59 cm

121
Colin Davidson
Study of Ed Sheeran 1
2015-19
oil on linen
41 x 38 cm

PORTRAITS BY COLIN DAVIDSON

A couple of weeks after Colin visited Suffolk, I returned to Belfast. Colin met me at the Ulster Museum to show me his portrait of the Irish poet Seamus Heaney, which had recently been put on display: the last portrait of the great man. He also took me into his exhibition *Silent Testimony,* which features a series of 18 large portraits of people of all ages and backgrounds who are connected by their individual experiences of loss during the Troubles In Northern Ireland. The exhibition was packed with people, some wiping away tears as they read the descriptive texts accompanying each painting. There was absolute silence in the gallery. The exhibition and the response of its audience powerfully expressed the profound and lasting impact of the Troubles on those left behind.

I asked Colin why his portraits are always the same size. He said that he sees everyone as equal, whether famous or unknown, and that our common humanity is central to his art. So he contains all his sitters, whoever they are, on the same sized canvas. Keeping the *Silent Testimony* portraits all the same size binds individual experience into a collective whole. This is an exhibition for all - 'the injured, their families, the families of those who had died and the wider community.' It is also, he said, for all communities around the world who have suffered loss through conflict.

Some weeks later, Colin started to work on his Ed Sheeran portraits. Using the quick pencil sketches and photographs as references, he began to create three large conte crayon drawings, showing Ed's face close-up, from slightly different angles (115, 117, 118). Each drawing is made to test whether its likeness is accurate enough to be successfully translated into a painting. They are energetic hatched and cross-hatched reconstructions of Ed's head and face. It is the abstract possibilities that keep each image alive with incident and the eye alert to the contrasts: of soft and strong line; of light and dark; of stillness and movement; and of hardness of form and delicacy of touch. You can imagine a sculptor using these drawings to work from. Colin sees them as visual recordings of the private Ed; the thoughtful, feeling Ed; the Ed the public never sees, but might hear in one of his quiet, reflective songs.

Colin also produced five small oil studies which directly resulted from the session in Suffolk (121-125). He describes them as 'like little sparks of time, little things Ed did.' Each captures a momentary experience and expresses the immediacy and spontaneity of Colin's creative encounter with his sitter. There is Ed looking down and reading, boldly painted but conventional (121). There is an unusual image of Ed with his eyes closed - not because he is asleep, but because Colin has asked him to close his eyes for a few seconds, to relax the face, and then to open them (123). The sudden movement of the muscles activates the face, and makes it comes alive in an instant. But this time, unusually, Colin opted for the eyes-closed image. He saw in it a strong visual metaphor for the internalised Ed: closed off and immersed in his own thoughts and feelings. In a third oil study, Ed looks out of a window, his face illuminated by a strong natural light which plays over the fullness and fleshiness of his form (122).

122
Colin Davidson
Study of Ed Sheeran 2
2015-19
oil on linen
41 x 38 cm

123
Colin Davidson
Study of Ed Sheeran 3
2015-19
oil on linen
41 x 38 cm

PORTRAITS BY COLIN DAVIDSON

The two final oil studies are very different in character from the previous three (124, 125). They are furiously worked and clearly not about trying to capture a likeness. Yet, having known Ed all his life, I can easily recognise him in them, despite the intentionally crude visual ingredients Colin uses. In one, Colin has scratched 'ED' into the wet paint in the top left corner, with the pointed end of his paint brush (124). There is something strong and definite about this portrayal. He no longer presents a passive Ed, but someone charged with emotional intensity. The furious nature of the painting style evokes angst, which is also betrayed by those deep, dark eyes. It is less a portrait of what Ed looks like, and more about what he himself feels like, or what Colin senses he is like. Colin employs a much more aggressive visual language to suggest an intense synergy between painter and musician. I hope a larger interpretation of this theme might emerge one day.

Colin eventually decided to use two of his drawings as the bases for separate large paintings, working on both canvases at the same time. He used the traditional grid method to transfer each drawing on to the canvas. Using the rapid sketches and photographs made in Suffolk as visual aids, he then started to work on each painting, building it up layer by layer. He had to wait for each layer to dry before starting the next. It is remarkable that with such a time-consuming process, the resulting paintings can appear so spontaneous and spirited.

I asked Colin what he sought to achieve with the large portraits (126, 128). 'I want the viewer to experience what I felt; how I related to Ed. If I never saw Ed again, I would remember him through his eyes. We communicate through our eyes, so I spent more time on that part of his face than anywhere else.' The eyes are finely painted with the analytical description of a miniaturist (129). Their stillness and focus suggest someone lost in their thoughts, oblivious to our presence. Despite the bravura of the painterly style all around, it is the eyes that hold the viewer. The dynamism of the image relies on the tension between clarity and incoherence. This is perfectly expressed in the contrast between the coolness, purity and precision of Ed's blue eyes and the wildness and fiery energy of his golden hair and beard. 'The two portraits describe the essence of Ed,' Colin explains. 'As a person, and in his life and work, Ed needs moments of clarity and moments of just being spontaneous. These paintings are about the tension between the two.'

124
Colin Davidson
Study of Ed Sheeran 4
2015-19
oil on linen
41 x 38 cm

125
Colin Davidson
Study of Ed Sheeran 5
2015-19
oil on linen
41 x 38 cm

126
Colin Davidson
Ed Sheeran 2016 (detail)
oil on linen, 127 x 117 cm
National Portrait Gallery, London

PORTRAITS BY COLIN DAVIDSON

I talked to Colin about the scale of his heads. Why are they so large? He explained that he saw no point in simply reproducing a head life-size. 'If it is larger than life, you have the opportunity for the head to become something else other than simply an accurate record. I like to explore elements of landscape in my portraits. I love the rhythm of brushwork, and to paint expressively without describing anything. My portraits are an amalgam of all sorts of experiences: of things seen, felt and imagined.'

Colin also spoke to me about how he wanted the viewer to be confronted by the portrait, to interact with it and be caught in its timelessness. The viewer, he said, is an essential part of the creative equation. The portrait is the catalyst. It is the viewer who 'completes' the painting by engaging with it and bringing their own feelings and interpretation to it. It is, he said, the same with Ed's songs, which affect millions of people around the world in different, individual, personal ways.

Colin completed the two portraits in early December 2016. One was acquired by the National Portrait Gallery, London (126). Both Colin and Ed attended a media unveiling of it in early May 2017. The portrait then went on display and has been popular with visitors ever since. The Gallery later reproduced it on an illuminated poster with the strapline 'Come in. Meet the locals.'

The other portrait (128) was acquired for a private collection and is being shown for the first time in the Ipswich exhibition, along with the three large drawings and five oil studies.

127
Illuminated poster of Colin Davidson's
2016 portrait of Ed Sheeran
National Portrait Gallery, London 2019
(photo John Sheeran)

128
Colin Davidson
Ed Sheeran II 2016 (detail)
oil on linen
127 x 117 cm

130
Colin Davidson
Ed Sheeran II 2016 (detail)
oil on linen
127 x 117 cm

131
Mark Surridge
Making Lego in the Dressing Room,
Switzerland, European Tour, 9 March 2012
(detail)

ED SHEERAN MADE IN SUFFOLK

PHOTOGRAPHS

by Mark Surridge

Mark Surridge started his career in the music industry as a tour manager for Example. He started to take photographs of gigs and life on the road. He first met Ed Sheeran when Ed was Example's support act on his UK tour in 2010. Mark joined Ed's European tour in 2012 and he has been photographing him ever since. He has documented key moments in Ed's career, notably his first three solo Wembley shows in 2015. He has also taken portrait shots of Ed which have been reproduced worldwide.

PHOTOGRAPHS BY MARK SURRIDGE

I have looked through hundreds of photographs of Ed taken by Mark Surridge but my favourite does not even show him. It was taken at the Allstate Arena, Chicago on 16 September 2017, in the early months of Ed's mammoth ÷ (Divide) world tour (133). The gig has just started and Ed has stepped on stage but we do not see him. Mark is more interested in the crowd. So he stands by the front barrier, with his lens right up close to some fans. He clicks away but no one notices him. They are totally focused on what is happening on stage. I imagine it is the moment Ed opens the gig with his 'love song for Suffolk', the hugely popular *Castle on the Hill*. Mark homes in on two fans - a woman and a boy. We do not know their relationship. Is it mother and child, or sister and younger brother? They both fill the picture space, and it is their reactions, and those around them, that he is most interested in.

You can just make out that the woman is wearing one of Ed's tour merchandise T-shirts under her unzipped hoodie. On it, you can get a glimpse of a bit of Ed: his tattooed arm, and his hand gripping his guitar. She is overwhelmed. Her hands are pressed tightly over her mouth to contain her emotions. Alongside, the boy has the look of sheer delight on his face, as if Father Christmas has just turned up. He is wide-eyed, and open-mouthed. This is a boy who smiles with his eyes. Behind them are two women; one smiling, the other cheering. The one on the left holds up her mobile phone to record the moment. It glows with light from the stage. There are out-of-focus sparkling lights from other phones behind. They seem to float in space and give a carnival atmosphere to the scene.

Yet, amidst all the highly-charged atmosphere, a man stands to the left, static. He shows no physical or emotional reaction. He holds a drink in his right hand. It will be a while, you sense, before he will engage with the 'Ed Sheeran experience', if at all. One of Ed's jobs this evening is to target this man and to convert him, and the many hundreds like him: the boyfriends, the husbands and the fathers.

You might argue that Mark Surridge simply struck lucky with this image. Anyone could have taken it if they were there at that moment. But I do not think anyone would have taken it, because most people do not possess Mark's instinct for the telling visual narrative, and certainly would not be able respond in an instant to something that will only last seconds.

I wondered where this visual instinct had come from. When I first met Mark in 2010 he was working as a tour manager for the rapper and singer Example, who was one of the first people to help Ed by taking him on his UK tour as his support act. I had no idea Mark had any interest in photography. But when he joined Ed's European tour in 2012, I noticed him in the background snapping away. When Mark came to Suffolk to discuss this exhibition, we sat for many hours talking about his life and work. He told me that he was born in Wiesbaden, Germany, and that his father had been a cameraman and had set up a production company in Germany, working mostly in TV. His father left home when Mark was three years old, and his mother and family returned to London, moving to Norbury and later Streatham, where Mark grew up. Mark often returned to Germany to visit his father. He remembers sitting on film sets and in editing studios studying him at work and learning how films were made. His father was also interested in photography and Mark recalls him converting a toilet at his home into a dark room.

132
Mark Surridge
*Making Lego in the Dressing Room,
Switzerland, European Tour,
9 March 2012* (detail)

133
Mark Surridge
Ed Comes on Stage,
Allstate Arena, Chicago, Illinois USA,
World Tour 16 September 2017

PHOTOGRAPHS BY MARK SURRIDGE

Years later, Mark worked with Jonathan Pearson, a close friend since primary school days, making music videos and short films. Pearson went on to direct the award-winning Channel 4 series *Run* and then joined UNIT9 and established an international reputation as a commercials director. During this time, Mark also worked alongside acclaimed director Luke Biggins, producing numerous music videos of the burgeoning Hip hop and Grime scenes in London and further afield. Long before the days of YouTube, many of these videos featured on Channel U, which championed unsigned acts. Some of the more memorable videos included Crazy Titch's *Singalong* (2004), S.A.S's *Cheerio* (2005) and Sway's *Up Ur Speed* (2006). He also worked on Kill Kenada's *In Your Throat* (2007), one of the first videos shot by Emil Nava, who would go on to direct several Ed Sheeran videos.

By 2006, Mark was working with the rapper and singer Professor Green, who introduced him to Example. Both were support acts for Plan B's *Who Needs Action When You Got Words* tour that year. In 2007, Professor Green and Example joined The Streets' *The Highland Tour* as support acts, for which Mark was tour manager. He was frequently asked to take photos and started to document the tour. Some of his photos of a gig or behind-the-scenes were printed up the next day and sold as posters to fans. He showed me a superb shot he took of Mike Skinner of The Streets crowd-surfing. Mark then joined Example on his tours for the next five years and started to take his photography much more seriously. He took photographs every day, not just of the music scene he was immersed in, but also of family and friends. He began to take an interest in portrait

photography too, which is something he now excels in. His portraits of Ed, Stormzy and others are highly regarded within the music industry and by the media, and have been used a great deal for promotional purposes.

I explained to Mark that I was keen to put together a group of his photos of Ed for the exhibition that told not just Ed's story, but Mark's story too. For we see Ed through Mark's eyes, through Mark's lens and through Mark's aesthetic sensibility. I also wanted the selection to reveal what Ed, his team and his fans all experience. Of all the photographers who have worked with Ed, Mark is one of the most trusted. Mark goes back in Ed's career much further than most. Ed gives him access to aspects of his life and career that no one else has.

The earliest photograph I selected for the exhibition shows a sound-check taking place at The Docks nightclub in the St Pauli district of Hamburg, Germany, during Ed's European tour in early 2012 (134). This was taken in the days when Ed was playing to around 1,000 people and was accompanied by just three or four people in his team – his manager, tour manager, sound engineer and a driver. Today he performs to stadiums of up to 90,000 people, and there can be 100 people in his tour team. So here is Ed in his early days as a pop star, in jeans and a hoodie, tuning his own guitar, with a basic loop pedal at his feet. Chris Marsh, Ed's sound man, is standing alongside. He has worked on every Ed Sheeran tour since and is now one of the most respected production managers in the world. The activity in this photo, taken in the afternoon, is not particularly interesting. I can imagine Mark, who was working as a temporary tour manager

134
Mark Surridge
*Soundcheck, Germany
European Tour
March 2012*
(detail)

135
Mark Surridge
Pre-Show Press, Mercedes
Benz Arena, Shanghai
China, World Tour
7 March 2015

136
Mark Surridge
Stuart Camp and Ed
Production Office, Mall
of Asia Arena, Manila
Philippines, World Tour
12 March 2015

at the time, walking through the darkened nightclub, seeing them on stage, and immediately realising what a wonderful smoky, atmospheric, timeless quality the scene had.

The exhibition includes an image of Ed's experience of the media, and theirs of him (135). It was taken during promo a few hours before a show at the Mercedes-Benz Arena in Shanghai, China, during a world tour in 2015. Mark remembers how surprised Ed's tour manager, Mark Friend, had been by the numbers of people who turned up. He stands in the centre of the scene, letting matters take their course. He had been told it would just be four or five people. Mark Surridge recalls the intensity of the tour, 'We were doing so much travelling, to so many countries and cities, that sometimes I was so tired I didn't really know where we were or what was going on. I would come across a scene like this every day, wondering how on earth Ed coped with it. He just sits there, patient, relaxed and smiling, while semi-organised chaos is all around.'

The exhibition features another telling behind-the-scenes shot on the same world tour (136). This time we are at the Mall of Asia Arena, in Bay City, Pasay, Philippines. Ed and his manager, Stuart Camp, are shown in the tour production office, which has been set up in a basketball team dressing room. The open suitcase, scattered papers, laptops, bottles of water, cans and unfinished pizzas show the unglamorous life on tour. This is about as un-rock-and-roll as it gets. Ed's team will be in and out of this space as soon as they can, after dealing with hundreds of matters, some unexpected, but most forgotten about as soon

as they reach the next city on the tour, when a new set of challenges will rear its head. Reading the body language and expressions of Stuart and Ed, it is clear that they have received information about something serious, but we will never know quite what. Mark has come across similar situations. The demands made on Ed, he says, are extraordinary. 'Stuart is a master at playing the middle-man; and he is the world expert at saying, "No." Thank God he is. He is also a bubble of sanity around Ed.' We can see part of an arm and fist resting on the table in the bottom left hand corner. The viewer gets a remarkable sense of actually being there, in this room, with Ed and Stuart, experiencing the tension.

As you would expect, Mark is fascinated by the many possible photographic treatments of the experience of Ed on stage. We see what Ed himself experiences, or the fans close to him, or those who can only see him as a dot from the top of a stadium, while the dot plays to a sea of humanity. In a shot taken by the stage at the Adelaide Entertainment Centre, Australia, we see Ed close up from below, standing on one of his sound monitors (137). He is belting out one of his songs. Mark later said, 'I like this shot. You get three Eds for the price of one! You see him from different angles, which is intriguing. The spotlights are dipped to the stage and strong light plays through the smoke. I like the way Ed's head is profiled against an intense veil of light. My favourite part of the picture is the shadow of his hand on the white T-shirt. It's a beautiful detail. Most people might not notice it, but I do. I think that this image works so much better in black and white than colour. The contrasts of light and dark, which help create the special atmosphere, are that much stronger.'

PHOTOGRAPHS BY MARK SURRIDGE

In a photograph taken at the Spotlight, BOK Center in Tulsa, Oklahoma, Mark captures a classic image of the artist in the spotlight: the troubadour singer-songwriter, walking and strumming (138). This could be Ed in a bar, or a club, early in his career when he played countless unpaid gigs. We cannot see the arena or audience, though we sense the figure is in the vastness of an open space. A single spotlight illuminates the far side of Ed, so that from our viewpoint we see him in profile, outlined by the light. Look closely and you will see that the light transforms his checked shirt into a beautiful pulse of red, yellow and blue, which trickles down his back.

In the Barclays Center, Brooklyn, New York City, Ed is shown in full flow (140). He is contorted, hand firmly on thigh, steadying himself as he lets rip. The face and neck muscles strain and his eyes are closed. We can make out some of the imagery on his tattooed arms, which includes a line drawing by Matisse of a mother and child (a favourite artwork of his mother, Imogen). A sequence of three floating boxing gloves pays homage to his grandfather, Bill Sheeran, who helped run British professional boxing from the 1960s to the 1980s. The gloves also refer to one of his career highlights - playing three sold-out shows during his first album tour in 2013 at Madison Square Garden, New York City, the home of American boxing. Ed is totally immersed in the performance, seemingly unaware of the audience. Mark catches all this in a single compelling image of Ed's isolation and total self-absorption. We see the lights of mobile phones recording him from distant seats, like fireflies in the night. Ed later told me that Beyoncé and Jay-Z were sitting in the front row, the first time they had seen him perform, so he made sure he gave his all for them.

In another shot, Mark shows us what the Ed Sheeran gig experience is like for the standing punters (142). He pushes into the crowd, 20 metres from the stage, looking up at Ed who is framed by the out-of-focus upraised hands of a fan in front of him. The multi-spot circular lights above him arc across the dark background like a magnified constellation. Mark comments, 'I wanted to be amongst the masses of people enjoying themselves to see what all the fuss was about. Ed has an extraordinary command and control of his audience. One minute they are clapping and dancing; the next they are wrapped up in each other, slowly swaying to an acoustic love song. It is remarkable to witness and to be part of.'

In another photograph, taken at the Valley View Casino Center in San Diego on the 2015 tour, Mark is fascinated by the lights and video screens suspended from far above the stage (139). He is attracted to the abstract confection of lines, shapes and colour in the vast space, especially the criss-cross beams of light, and the rectilinear screens with their vivid yellow and purple colours. Ed is picked out by a distant spotlight, as if adopting the pose of a classical sculpture on a plinth. In another image, which Mark took at Red Rocks in Morrison, near Denver, Colorado, we get to see Ed performing in a unique, dramatic natural amphitheatre, well-known for its perfect acoustic surroundings (141). Mark described it to me as a 'primal' place. Two vast rock cliffs glow like golden monoliths. They frame the huge crowd, which can be identified by the thousands of twinkling lights from mobile phones. Ed, his guitar slung around his back and his arms raised high, acknowledges the cheers of the crowd. To the right someone holds up a large neon heart.

137
Mark Surridge
Triple Ed, Adelaide Entertainment Centre Australia, World Tour 2 April 2015
(detail)

138
Mark Surridge
Ed in the Spotlight, BOK Center
Tulsa, Oklahoma, USA, World Tour
9 May 2015

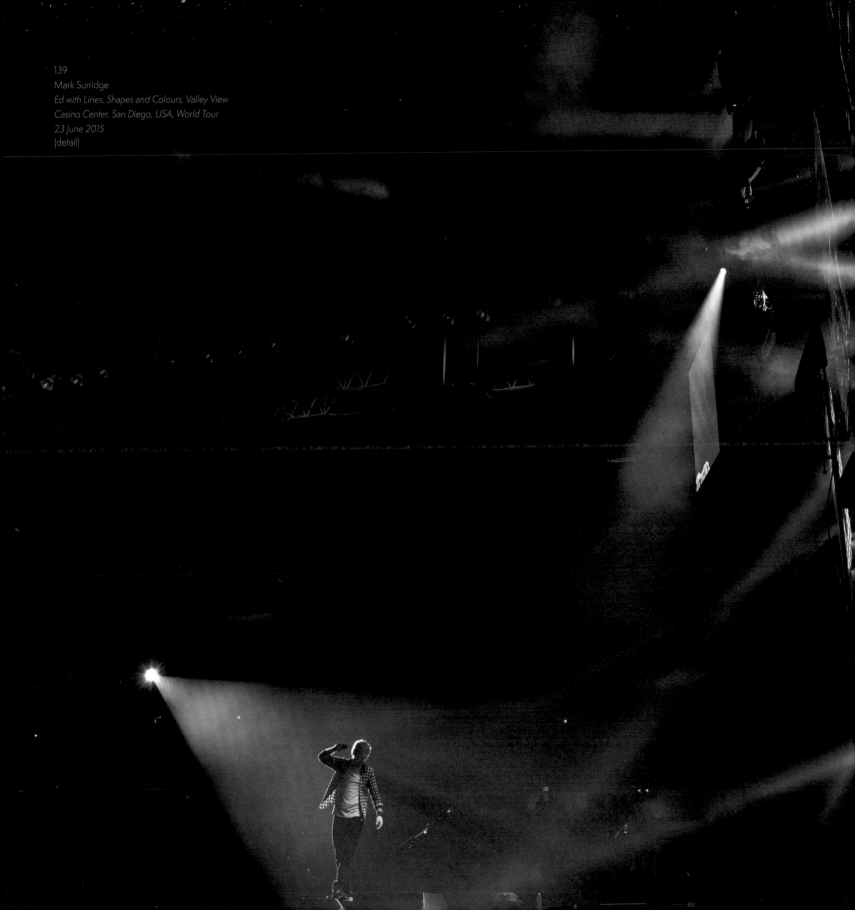

139
Mark Surridge
Ed with Lines, Shapes and Colours, Valley View
Casino Center, San Diego, USA, World Tour
23 June 2015
(detail)

PHOTOGRAPHS BY
MARK SURRIDGE

I think the greatest challenge in Ed's touring career so far was to play Wembley Stadium for the first time entirely solo in July 2015. No one had ever attempted this before. He was booked for three sell-out nights, performing to a quarter of a million people. He asked Mark to document the Wembley shows, both on stage and off. Mark shot hundreds of pictures and I have chosen five (144-148) that I think capture the uniqueness of the occasion and some extraordinary moments of tension, beauty and calm that Mark witnessed.

The first captures the anxiety and nervousness of Ed and his team just before he goes on stage (144). He is waiting in the underbelly of Wembley, surrounded by his manager, Stuart Camp, his tour manager, Mark Friend, his promoter, Stuart Galbraith, who is mostly hidden from view, and two of his security detail, Mickey and John. Ed looks down and scratches his head. His concerned expression betrays intense focus on the task at hand, and the enormous pressure he is under. No one says a word, and all try to look away, except Stuart Camp, who has worked with Ed for five years, and is well aware of what he is going through. Just moments away is a huge expectant audience. None of the group knows whether Ed will be able to carry off the biggest night of his life. Mark later commented to me, 'This was the first time I ever saw Ed nervous. It was a big thing for all of them. Wembley is Wembley whoever you are. It's the national stadium. We were all thinking "You can't mess this one up".'

140
Mark Surridge
Ed Giving it Everything, Barclays Center
New York City, USA, World Tour
31 May 2015
(detail)

141
Mark Surridge
Ed at Red Rocks Amphitheatre
Morrison, Colorado, USA, World Tour
30 June 2015
(detail)

PHOTOGRAPHS BY MARK SURRIDGE

The next image shows Ed on an enormous stage at Wembley, with huge speakers and lights suspended from a vast tented roof structure rising 100 feet above the stage (145). I remember the incredible roar of the crowd as he came on stage. The photograph shows him as a tiny figure facing an enormous crowd, one of the largest he had ever experienced. My wife Imogen and I were in seats at the half-way line, our stomachs churning away at the thought of the daunting challenge facing him. The sea of people in front of us was a staggering sight. We could only imagine what it must have been like for Ed. Weirdly, I feel nervous even now looking at Mark's photograph. But as soon as Ed came on stage and started his first song, he got into his stride, and the evening just shot by. Mark later recalled the experience, 'Wembley really brought it home to me. Just one man controlling so many people. I felt it was like a huge cult gathering. Ed asked them to sing and they sang! I thought at the time that there can't be a drug known to man that can give you a feeling like that. I felt it too. I got such a buzz from just being there and watching him.'

The third of Mark's photographs of Wembley in 2015, taken on the second night, captures the simplicity of Ed's act: just a guitar, two microphones and a loop station are all it requires to entertain over 80,000 people (146). But I also love this picture for its beauty: the colour scheme of white, black and blue; the electric blue line that seems to bind Ed like a ribbon to the stadium and the crowd; the thousands of lights, each representing a person engaging with Ed's song. We catch a glimpse of the famous Wembley arch at the top of the picture, with the pitch floodlights below. The dark mirror-like staging reflects the stage lights as a patchwork of bright squares and is freckled by the reflected dots of light from the crowd. A lone empty plastic water bottle lies on the stage floor.

In the fourth Wembley photograph, Ed sits alone in his dressing room, having just come off stage (147). Usually, he does not allow anyone in, not even his family. This is the private and solitary time he needs to wind down and relax. But Mark is given access. Ed leans back on a Union Jack sofa, smoking a roll-up, ashtray alongside, a plastic water bottle in his hand, and a towel around his neck. His checked shirt is soaked with his sweat, after an energetic two hours on stage. Ed has been given the England football team's changing room as his own dressing room. There are brand new England football shirts on hangers, with football boots below, in the England players' changing spaces. They are a gift to Ed and his team from the then England captain, Wayne Rooney, who is a friend of Ed's. The number 10 shirt has Ed's surname on the back.

In the final Wembley photograph from 2015, it feels as though we are actually on stage with Ed. He is playing the intro to his huge hit *Thinking Out Loud* on the electric guitar (148). I selected this image because it is one of Mark's favourite shots of Ed. Mark describes the scene, 'He is in his own zone, deep into the music. He could be at the Waterfront in Norwich or a pub in Ipswich. He is not fazed in the slightest by the setting or the immensity of the crowd. It's just him, his guitar, his loop pedal, the set-list on the floor, a few bottles of water, cups and a towel. It takes extraordinary confidence to do what he does.'

PHOTOGRAPHS BY MARK SURRIDGE

In August 2016, Imogen and I were lucky to be invited to the Abbey Road Studios, London to watch our sons, Matthew and Ed, working on the recording of a fully orchestral version of Ed's song *Perfect*. Matthew had orchestrated the song and Ed sang it live. It was such a privilege to be there with our boys, and to be in the studio where the Beatles worked. Ed asked Mark to document the whole day. I have included a photo which Mark took from the stairs leading up to the sound production room (149). This is a team photo looking down on the conductor and musicians in the orchestra, and a line of figures at the back, which includes Ed, Matthew, sound engineers, cameramen and other musicians.

As already mentioned, Mark is an accomplished portrait photographer, so I have included one of his professional press photo shoot images of Ed, which was taken in Chicago in 2017 in a makeshift studio Mark had set up next to Ed's dressing room (143). 'Ed and I were messing around, as he'd just got a new leather jacket. I wanted to get more than just a standard portrait of him, so I asked him to pull the jacket up around his head, with the zipped wings either side of his face. It was done as a bit of a joke. Ed as a dark, brooding character. Not his persona at all. But it worked and so I kept it. I used a Canon 5D Mark 4 camera, which I use for most of my work. It was taken with a 50mm lens, which has a fixed focal length and is just right for this type of close-up. I like the stillness of the pose, the piercing eyes and the wavy, dishevelled hair.'

In June 2018, Ed returned to play four nights at Wembley Stadium during his ÷ *(Divide)* world tour. On the third night, while singing *Shape of You* as his encore, he brought Stormzy on. Wembley erupted. And Mark captured the moment, close up (150). Ed and Stormzy are good friends and have great respect for each other. You can see how much the two of them are enjoying themselves. The amazing psychedelic sheets of colour and spiralling leaf and rose forms on the huge video screens perfectly complement the festival party atmosphere in the stadium at the time. It is an image of joyful positivity, and a perfect one to complete Mark's section of the exhibition.

143
Mark Surridge
Press Photo Shoot, Pre-Show,
Allstate Arena, Chicago, Illinois, USA,
World Tour
16 September 2017

144
Mark Surridge
Ed About to Go on Stage
First Night Wembley Stadium
London, England
10 July 2015 (detail)

145
Mark Surridge
First Night at Wembley Stadium
London, England
10 July 2015
(detail)

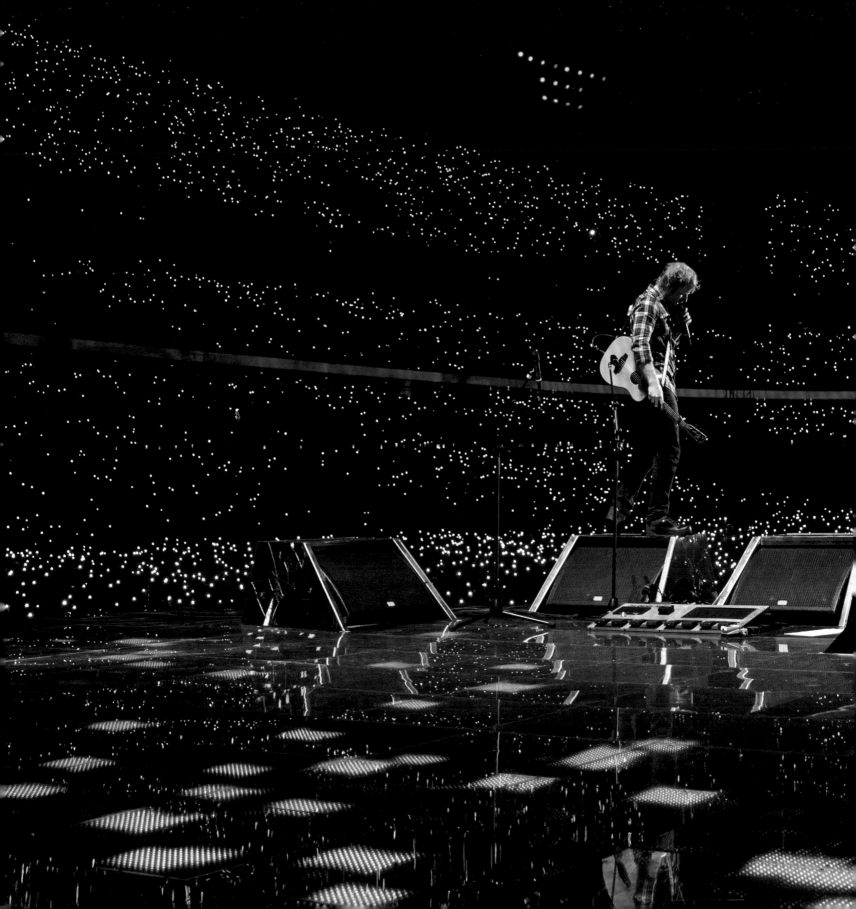

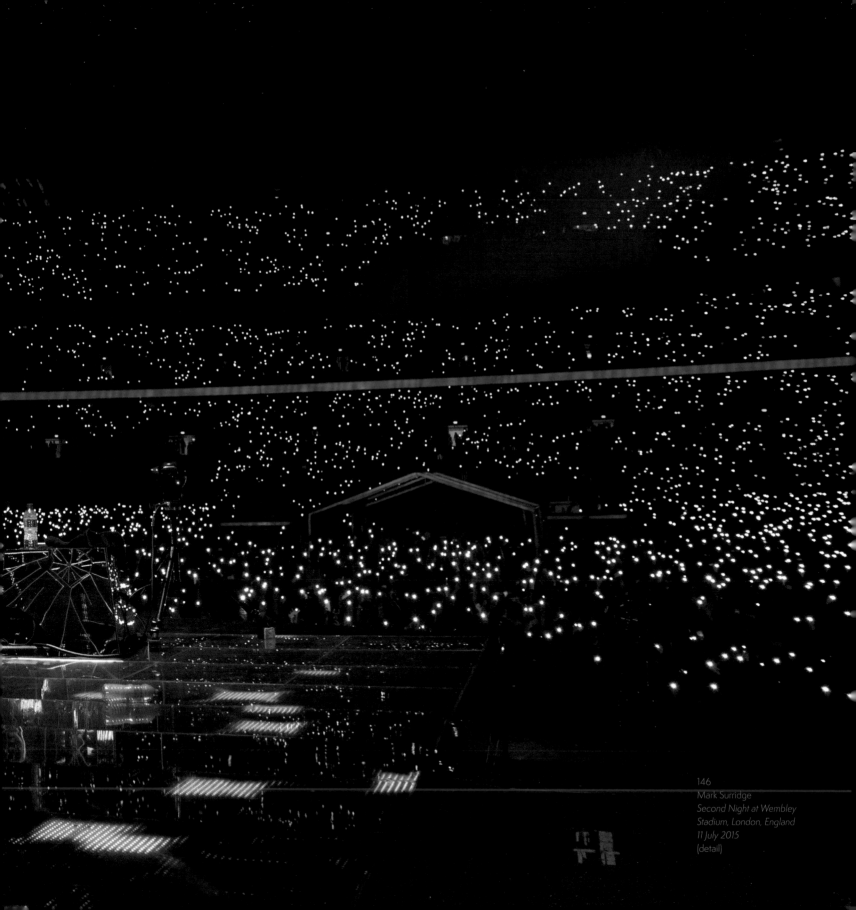

146
Mark Surridge
*Second Night at Wembley
Stadium, London, England
11 July 2015*
(detail)

148
Mark Surridge
*Third Night at Wembley
Stadium, London, England
12 July 2015*

149
Mark Surridge
Group Photo after Recording Perfect
Abbey Road Studios, London
5 August 2016
(detail)

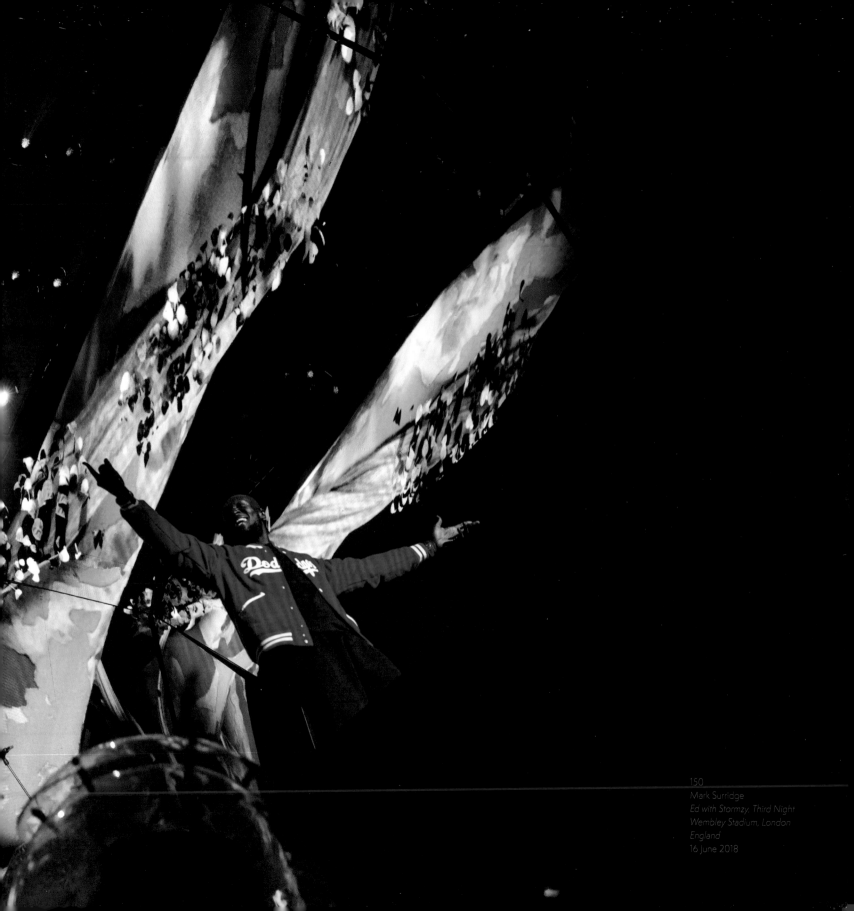

150
Mark Surridge
Ed with Stormzy, Third Night
Wembley Stadium, London
England
16 June 2018

JOHN SHEERAN

John Sheeran is the father of Ed Sheeran. He has worked for 40 years in the arts. He was a fine art museum curator during the 1980s, including seven years as Curator of The Dulwich Picture Gallery, London - England's first purpose-built public art gallery. John then ran Sheeran Lock Ltd with his wife, Imogen, for 20 years. They organised numerous art exhibitions and education projects in the UK and around the world. These included *Travels with the Prince* at Hampton Court Palace in 1998 to mark the 50th birthday of Prince Charles, and *Our World in the Year 2000* at the UN Headquarters in New York, which featured paintings by 250 artists from 50 countries. In 2008, John started to give art lectures in Suffolk. His first series, *Discover the Great Painters*, comprised 80 lectures on his favourite Western European artists from the 13th Century to the present.